SUCCESSFUL MANAGEMENT CONSULTING
Building a Practice with Smaller Company Clients

W. M GREENFIELD

PRENTICE-HALL, INC., Englewood Cliffs, New Jersey 07632

Library of Congress Cataloging-in-Publication Data

Greenfield, W. M
 Successful management consulting.

 Bibliography: p.
 Includes index.
 1. Business consultants. 2. Small business.
I. Title.
HD69.C6G72 1987   658.4'6   86-30494
ISBN 0-13-863143-3 (c)
ISBN 0-13-863135-2 (p)

Editorial/production supervision and
 interior design: David Ershun/Nancy Menges
Cover design: Lundgren Graphics, Ltd.
Manufacturing buyer: Carol J. Bystrom

For Joe, the best kind of consultant

The publisher offers discounts on this book when ordered in bulk
quantities. For more information, write:

 Special Sales/College Marketing
 Prentice-Hall, Inc.
 College Technical and Reference Division
 Englewood Cliffs, NJ 07632

Printed in the United States of America

10 9 8 7 6 5 4 3 2 1

ISBN   0-13-863143-3   025   {C}
ISBN   0-13-863135-2   025   {P}

PRENTICE-HALL INTERNATIONAL (UK) LIMITED, *London*
PRENTICE-HALL OF AUSTRALIA PTY. LIMITED, *Sydney*
PRENTICE-HALL CANADA INC., *Toronto*
PRENTICE-HALL HISPANOAMERICANA, S.A., *Mexico*
PRENTICE-HALL OF INDIA PRIVATE LIMITED, *New Delhi*
PRENTICE-HALL OF JAPAN, INC., *Tokyo*
PRENTICE-HALL OF SOUTHEAST ASIA PTE. LTD., *Singapore*
EDITORA PRENTICE-HALL DO BRASIL, LTDA., *Rio de Janeiro*

CONTENTS

PREFACE

This book is not the compleat "how to" for becoming a consultant. It does not start by telling you what business is, what consulting is, what a big business consulting is, or how much money you might theoretically be able to make as a consultant. Frankly, if that is what you seek, this book is not for you. (Before you put it down, however, you might check the reading list provided in Appendix A.)

This book assumes you have some notion about what you are doing (or are about to do). You know you are interested in consulting. You know some basic facts—that proposals are important to a consulting business, that pricing and politics are important and that initial client interviews are often crucial. It also assumes you know the areas(s) in which you (will) consult and are good at doing the project work. I will not waste your time with that information: you will not have to skip chapters in this book.

You are, in fact, probably doing some consulting now. What you want are two basic things: ways to do it better and ways to get the business side of your business more together—more businesslike, if you will. *Those* are the purposes of this book.

More to the point, this book focuses on a segment of the consulting business that tends to get lost in most business/consulting books. Most books about either business or consulting (or both) appear to assume that all companies are large and structured along divisional lines. They implicitly assume that small companies are similar except in size. They further assume that the goal of all smaller companies is to become larger so that they can look and operate like their giant relatives.

The fact is that most companies are not huge. Most are not organized by divisions. Most companies are small and have ambitions to grow only into larger small companies. Few owners really intend to be running General Motors–sized operations within their lifetimes. Those of us who work with smaller and/or newer companies know that the size and operations assumptions built into most discussions of business and consulting are (1) not true and (2) seriously destructive as a mind set for consultants who work or hope to work with such smaller companies.

This book avoids those traps by adopting a clear focus on smaller companies. It explicitly states its assumptions about the sizes and structures of these companies. Most important, it addresses the issues of how working with such companies differs from working with corporate giants. I offer you, as a consultant to smaller companies, the specific kinds of information you need to offer better service to these companies, to build a true practice based on your work with them, and to be more confident about what you are doing and how you are doing it.

WHAT IS A *SMALLER COMPANY* FOR PURPOSES OF THIS BOOK?

The notion of *smaller* in this book is based more on operating and ownership characteristics than on annual sales or numbers of employees. The essential issue is who really runs the company and how he or she organizes the work of the company.

The companies discussed here are mainly owner-operated. They may have other owners besides the one who is the operating manager. It is likely, however, that at least some of the other (theoretically nonoperating) owners may be family members and/or old family friends. Needless to say, family concerns are frequently brought into the business arena.

In this kind of company, ownership—and the particular personalities of the owners—frequently affects the structure and staffing of the company. Few such companies are organized divisionally, for example. They are often informal, virtually unstructured, in organization. Often, a number of employees have been there since the company began. If the owner was more progressive than most, a number of these employees may hold some equity in the company.

But the hallmark of the kind of smaller company discussed in this book is the focus of leadership. In most companies that meet the foregoing description, only one person really makes decisions. Sometimes included in the decision making are long-time associates and/or close friends. Essentially, however, absolutely nothing happens unless Old Charlie (or Charlie's group) O.K.s it. Hires, down to the stock boy, may need to be approved. Purchases may have to be approved, down to the level of paper clips and petty cash. In short, despite the financial or employee size of the company, it is a one-man show or a committee-run operation.

In some senses, in fact, Ford Motor Company under the sole direction of Henry would have qualified as "smaller," as defined here, since it was basically a one-man show. It operated like a giant small company rather than an average giant company. This is a rarity, however. Most firms that meet this definition of smaller are likely to have fewer than fifty employees. The number, of course, depends on the industry, since firms in capital-intensive industries, for example, have relatively few employees for their size in annual sales or in total assets. Because of such wide industry disparities, it is virtually impossible to assign a sales volume or asset investment cutoff point for *smaller* under this definition.

WHO COULD USE THIS BOOK

This book was written for people who work or wish to work on a consulting basis with smaller companies as defined here. The notion that smaller companies are fundamentally different from larger ones occurred to me one day as I was helping a large corporate client plan a new line of business. This client's concerns and priorities were different from those of my smaller-company clients. The methods of operation and organization were different. The frustrations of working with them were different—no less real or frustrating, but definitely different.

When a smaller company considers significantly expanding or changing a product line, for example, its first considerations are usually funds with which to finance the addition, personnel to staff it, and management to run it. All these are frequently considered in a cash-strapped atmosphere. The question is often how to get the same people to do more work or how to shift people to different work and reorganize the remainder. The overriding objective is usually keeping investments and cash outflows relatively small.

My corporate client approached everything from an almost diametrically opposed perspective. Their first move was to acquire a great deal of rather expensive leased space and a staff of four managers and a secretary dedicated solely to getting this project off the ground. (No one had yet adequately defined the project.) Although this was not necessarily either better or worse as an approach, it was definitely different from my smaller-company perspective.

Whenever I asked about cost, I was told, "It's in the budget"— as if it didn't really cost anything, because the money was already "spent." Whenever I asked about investment in equipment, I was told what it would cost on an annual (depreciation) basis. Clearly, it had not occurred to the managers that someone would actually have to *pay* for the gear before it could be depreciated. In short, these managers were insulated in many ways from the realities that most owners of smaller companies face daily.

These managers also had no major personal stake in the outcome of the project. One sensed that, on the whole, they would prefer for the project to succeed, but that this was mainly just part of the job. Although their jobs would undoubtedly change if the project was a total flop, and their raises might be affected if the product did not meet their projections, none of them believed that their livelihoods— let alone their business survival—hung on their success or failure in this particular project. This produced a laid-back attitude toward the project that was entirely foreign to me after all my years in smaller companies.

Owner–managers of smaller companies can never lose track of some essential realities—that development costs money, that failure is serious and perhaps fatal. If they need reminding, their bankers and creditors will remind them if I fail to do so. The sense that unavoidable reality may not be thoroughly enjoyable produces a mind set in smaller-business clients that sets them apart from the corporate clients we all learned about in the business books. Because of this attitude, a great many of the other things we all learned in business school or in our positions in larger corporations may not be particularly relevant in the smaller-company environment.

The purpose of this book, then, is to begin to identify areas in which the differences between larger and smaller companies constitute a real difference in the environment for consultants. My intent is to consider the implicatons of large/small company differences as they relate to selling consulting services to smaller companies and to performing well on smaller-company consulting projects. My aim is to replace large-company notions of what business and consulting are like with a more realistic (and, I hope, profitable) sense of what smaller-company consulting can and should be.

To this end, this book offers strategies and approaches that have been developed through years of consulting work with smaller-company clients. Since you, yourself, are operating as a smaller company through your consulting practice, this book also offers assistance in structuring your own business affairs so that they help, rather than get in the way of, your actual consulting work.

I hope you will be able to profit from my earlier errors and to make use, in your consulting practice, of some of the differences I have identified in working with larger and smaller company clients.

WHO AM I, ANYWAY?

What background can I offer that might make it worth your while to consider my advice in such sensitive areas?

My first real job (not counting such standard items as lifeguard, dining hall help, etc.) was with a classic smaller company. The president's wife was our bookkeeper. Staff included three other people and a part-timer in the mail area. There was always a real question about whether payroll checks would really show up on Friday. Once in a while they didn't—but I had a great title. The company is now larger and prosperous.

Since then most of my work has been in one kind of consulting or another. I worked for three years as assistant to the research director of a medium-sized consulting company. There I worked mainly with government and giant-company clients, including the World Bank and the Pharmaceutical Manufacturers Association. I then joined a larger company, Blue Shield of Massachusetts, Inc., where I served as manager of their internal consulting group for another three years.

At that point, it occurred to me that a staff position, even a good one, in a larger company would neither become what I wanted it to become nor be a real springboard to increased autonomy and responsibility. I decided to go to Harvard for an M.B.A. and to set up my own consulting business at the same time. (School was expensive, and one does have to eat.)

Since that time, except for a summer job as a staff auditor for a "Big Eight" accounting firm, I have developed and run my consulting practice. In addition to developing my practice and running the business, I also spent seven years teaching management (part-time) at the Boston University School of Management. I taught management strategy and was responsible for the development and teaching of a course in Management of Small Business. In the process of teaching that course, which dealt with new-ventures development, I worked with hundreds of students to help them develop their own business plans.

In the ten years my company has been operating, the focus of my practice has changed somewhat (as will be described further in Chapter 8). Its overall objectives, however—providing assistance only when needed, teaching the client as projects progress, and providing efficient service and good value to the client—have remained unchanged.

We have served large-company clients, including insurance companies, banks, associations, and government agencies. We have served smaller companies in such industries as media (print, film, broadcast), health services, job-shop-type manufacturing, and professional services. I derive the greatest enjoyment and sense of satisfaction from my smaller-company clientele. Working with such companies is definitely not boring.

Through this book, I hope to share some of the enjoyment and excitement with you. You will find client stories (anonymous, for obvious reasons) dotting this book. Through them, and through other stories about my consulting practice, you will learn a great deal more about me and my consulting experiences.

I sincerely hope you find this book useful and helpful. I would appreciate hearing any comments you might have about it or anything you might have to add to it. You can reach me directly at W.M Greenfield Associates, 455 Hope Street, 4E, Stamford, CT 06906.

Part I

SMALLER COMPANIES AND CONSULTANTS

1

SMALLER COMPANIES ARE NOT MINIATURE LARGE COMPANIES

This is a book about consulting to smaller companies. Those of you who are not intimately familiar with lots of smaller companies (or who have never given the matter much thought) are probably wondering why that needs a whole, separate book. After all, aren't there more books on how to do consulting than any sane human being would want to read?

Well, yes and no. Without even commenting on quality, consultants to smaller companies can be seriously misled by books touting methods and approaches appropriate to larger companies. At best, such methods may be merely useless and expensive. I recall, for example, a consultant who read that advertising and direct mail could sell a consulting practice. (In all fairness, the book *didn't* say that advertising and direct mail could sell consulting *projects*.) The consultant embarked on a print blitz. The book focused on image advertising with a general-specialty emphasis. Our consultant reasoned that his potential clients did not read many of the slick business magazines. Therefore, he developed his ads for the local papers, which they did read. People were somewhat puzzled, since that kind of ad rarely appeared in the business pages of local papers, sandwiched between bank rate ads and those for local computer stores. They also thought it rather odd that the consultant did not bring his message, whatever it was, to the area business discussion groups, where he could tell them in person. Although the consultant followed up with a direct mailing (as he was supposed to), his mailing piece still had to be rather general. It was, after all, going to many diverse business owners.

Some people did call him. Mainly, they wanted to know what he was selling. And *they* were largely people who already knew him and his company. The net result: no new business, at a fairly significant cost.

The book also said that questionnaires were great ways to generate and develop business. The process was supposed to work as follows. First, you pick a topic or series of topics related to your area of expertise. Next, you send out questionnaires to appropriate companies. You tabulate responses, do a quick-and-dirty analysis, and send the questionnaire and the results to your potential client list. Your cover letter relates the material to your consulting expertise and your probable ability to provide assistance to that kind of company.

Think about this process for a moment, though. Larger company managers have staff to deal with questionnaires. They are frequently interested in where they or their companies stand in relation to "average." They may even view such data as useful performance measures. Smaller companies, however, are perennially strapped for labor and time. How often do you think their owners fill out questionnaires on matters not of burning and immediate interest, from sources they don't know? Even assuming the responses come in, how many entrepreneurs do you know who care much what *anyone* else is doing? Will they take the time to read your study and analysis? Even if they read it, how many are likely to call, cold, to do business with your company? Enough to make the time and cost worthwhile? Doubtful.

Still another consultant almost went down the tubes following advice given in a how-to-do-consulting seminar. This seminar advanced newsletters as extremely useful business-generating tools. The idea was to put together snippets of useful information, plaster your or your company's name all over it, and ship copies to clients, former clients, and potential clients. (Perhaps you could add the results of your questionnaire?)

This consultant went to work on her newsletter. It cost a bundle, since it had to reflect (the seminar people said) an image appropriate to her intended level of consulting. She spent inordinate amounts of time and effort finding information, writing, researching a prospect list, and other such tasks. Admittedly, she went overboard. But by the time she had a really beautiful newsletter, she also had virtually no business. The newsletter was supposed to bring them in in droves, however, so it was OK.

Well, it didn't work out quite that way. This consultant did not happen to have a staff person to do the newsletter work (as do larger companies). She did it herself, which left no time for the more standard business development activities. She then belatedly noticed that, while most consulting business takes a long time to develop, smaller company consulting project development frequently takes even longer than that. She had also managed to create *one* issue of her newsletter. The seminar people had suggested one a month or one a quarter to keep your name before your market. As she surveyed the situation, our consultant concluded that she certainly could not manage this kind of newsletter approach on her own (and still eat).

The underlying problem with all this good advice is that, while it may work for larger companies, it fails to take into account the very real basic differences between larger and smaller companies. As the consultants discussed here found out to their detriment, they really *are* different, not just scaled down. Different—in some very fundamental ways.

The remainder of this chapter reviews a number of key areas of difference, highlighting those that will make a difference to you as you build a practice in consulting with smaller companies. Incidentally, it will give you a whole new slant on how-to-do-consulting books, helping you to assess what might really work, if modified appropriately, in your smaller company practice. The remainder of this book will help you to the insights and offer you the tools to make those modifications, should you decide to do so.

COMPANY DIFFERENCES

As you read through this section and, indeed, the rest of the book, please remember that not *all* smaller companies fit all the characteristics described. In fact, one of the most interesting things about smaller companies is that they tend to defy categorization. The purpose of these descriptions is thus not really to slot companies, but to help you understand what might be going on with your clients or potential clients when what is going on doesn't make much sense if viewed from the larger company perspective.

The differences about which you should be aware are those that relate to the companies themselves. These have been grouped into three subsections: structural differences, economic differences, and statistical differences. Given the nature of companies in general and of smaller companies in particular, categories will overlap and run together. The attempt to separate them has been made to facilitate understanding and analysis.

Structural Differences

Consider walking into most smaller companies and asking to see the current organization chart. The most likely response would be a blank stare. Odds are, nobody has ever bothered to make one. Why do it if everyone knows who to see for what? Perhaps more to the point, it would be difficult to make an organization chart because of the way responsibilities are divided up. It is rare, in a smaller company, for anyone to serve as a specialist in only one area. People frequently do a number of different things, either because they like it that way or because there are never enough people to go around. In the latter case, people develop new areas of skill simply because there is no other way to get things done.

Given this arrangement for accomplishing work, the resulting organization chart, should one try to draw it, would be a crazy quilt. Either lines would cross at odd angles, or the same name would appear in a number of boxes. Moreover, the names in the boxes would periodically shift, as one or another person added a new job or handed off an area of responsibility to another. In short, in smaller companies, there is less concern with whose job something is or with a person's job description and more emphasis on getting the job done—whatever (and whoever) it takes.

It follows from this discussion that smaller companies tend to look for a different kind of personnel than do larger companies and to evaluate them differently. While smaller companies seek expertise, they also value flexibility. They have to. A person who was aggressively a specialist in only one area would be unlikely really to become a part of the team in most smaller companies. He would also be less likely to feel comfortable in this kind of smaller company atmosphere.

These differences can be important to you in assessing the companies with which you hope to work or with which you are working. You cannot count, for example, on keeping specialty areas separate from one another. It is quite possible that the same guy will be involved in, or in fact running, a number of them at once. You cannot assume that you will be working with disparate departments or skill areas in a smaller company because they may well overlap. Depending on the type of project you are doing or offering, you may want to maintain your flexibility and modify your preferred approach as necessary.

Finally, and perhaps most important for those of us who do consulting with smaller companies, you cannot necessarily assume a high level of expertise in a specialty field. This, you will note, is not necessarily the result of poor hiring or managerial incompetence but rather may be the result of the fact that your area of primary concern is the second or third job for the person you are dealing with. She is learning, has learned a great deal, but has numerous other things to take care of. In this area, in particular, rather than bemoaning the fact that you do not have experts to work with, be overjoyed that someone (probably the owner) recognized that there was an "expertise gap" and brought you in to fill it (or that you offered to fill). Your role, under these circumstances, becomes as much (more?) that of teacher as that of doer or recommender. This theme recurs throughout this book.

Please note that these observations are stated as "things you cannot assume." This is simply a reminder that they might be true in a given company, despite the fact that they are frequently not true in smaller companies in general. The purpose of pointing them out is to permit you to consider the companies with which you propose to do business from more than one perspective as it relates to your project. It offers you more of that old smaller company requirement: flexibility.

Economic Differences

This represents perhaps the most obvious area of difference between smaller and larger companies. I state a few key items here, despite the fact that you have probably already figured them out.

In the economic area, smaller companies come closest to being miniature large companies. The effects of economic and financial smallness, however, are extremely disproportionate; that is, financial and economic difficulties increase almost geometrically with decreases in size. In some cases, the increases seem almost exponential. As a consultant to smaller companies, you need to be acutely aware of the constraints placed on smaller companies in these areas. Some of the areas most frequently affected include inventory and supply and credit operations. For example, a small auto rebuilder was forced to pay cash for his parts purchases, a factor that alone increased his costs by 30 percent. His problem was that he was too small to make the parts shipment minimums of most dealers.

Banks frequently react poorly to smaller companies, particularly those that do not intend to grow aggressively. To paraphrase Mark Twain, they are institutions that will lend you money if you can prove you don't need it. And smaller companies often really need it. Their main difficulty in this area is that the money they need is big enough to create a noticeable loss if not repaid but not large enough to hold out the promise of significant profit to the lender. When smaller companies *do* get loans, they tend to get them at relatively less favorable rates, as well—despite the fact that studies have shown that smaller company loans are less costly to service and collect than average business loans.

Such constraints seem to become part of the smaller company mindset in many instances. Owners and managers, recognizing the variability of their cash flows, will frequently do almost anything to avoid spending current money. They will sometimes not take on needed staff that they can afford now (and use to increase profit and profitability later) simply because they fear that they may not be able to pay them forever. This is not a rational response, and they usually recognize that. It is an emotional response, but you need to be aware of it because so many consulting recommendations involve using resources now for longer-term gain. Recognize that you may have to overcome emotional biases as well as the standard financial ones when you work with smaller companies.

These factors may also motivate you to devise innovative payment methods for your consulting fees. Such fees are often the ultimate in buying now for future gain. Anything you can do to soften the bite will make selling your services easier. This point is discussed further in later chapters.

Statistical Differences

Statistics abound about smaller companies. The key item is the fact that smaller companies fail or simply go out of business more often than larger ones. While you already know this, it is also something you need to be aware of as you work with smaller companies.

Cash shortages are survival issues when the banks do not routinely extend short-term credit lines. Shipping delays may be survival issues as well if your client's payment hangs on delivery of the product he was going to make with those shipments. He probably had little or no buffer stock. In short, you need to keep in mind that, although smaller companies tend to see survival threats in everything, much of the time those threats are real.

. . AND OWNERS ARE NOT JUST MANAGERS WITH EQUITY

Your work in smaller companies will probably be done for and with the owner of the company. And one of the most interesting features of this relationship will be the myriad ways you will discover in which owners are not managers with equity. The thing to remember is that your client probably *is* the company. She conceived it. She built it from nothing. She keeps it together and running. And, most important, she is (and feels) responsible for it in its entirety.

This owners' approach to a business creates a much more emotional attitude than obtains in larger companies—an ownership attitude toward everything that touches the business. I have spoken with owners who refused to believe that employees could be stealing or lying, for example. They believed that their company was a "family" and that their "children" could never do those things to them. When it is proved otherwise, these owners feel deep distress and betrayal, as opposed to financial injury.

This kind of paternalistic attitude isn't the only result of deep emotional involvement with the business, however. While a manager usually goes home at some standard hour except in emergencies (and under duress), owners often almost live with their businesses. They tend to take few vacations, little time off. Their businesses become second homes (and, given their divorce rates, often primary homes). Since they tend to see the process as personal rather than solely business, they expect their upper-level employees to follow suit. In short, they tend not to recognize that what is life to them can be merely a job to others who work for them.

These others from whom they expect total commitment often include their consultants and other outside contractors. Some of my clients have called me at 10 P.M. or on Sunday (or both), *assuming* that I had been working on their projects. (Being a small company owner myself, I frequently was.) These owners can become distressed if you cannot instantly recall tiny details or if you happen to be watching television or working on something for another company. Larger company managers are generally not working during non-working hours, and most do not expect their staff members to be living the company at all times.

While the emotional content of working with owners of smaller companies is frequently higher than working with larger company clients, real difficulties can occur when owners translate their ownership into power trips. Even when a larger company manager is also an equity holder, he rarely has enough clout to make totally independent decisions. What this manager wants, he may or may not get, but it is a negotiation process.

Smaller company owners, however, generally do have the power to make decisions all by themselves. Frequently, they are sole equity holders. They have always made all the decisions for their companies simply because there was nobody else to do it. This exercise of total power within the company becomes a habit. When coupled with a clear sense of the world's constraints, it may make for a very compassionate human being.

Even when an owner's use of power is constrained by reality, the existence of a unitary power source within a company can make life difficult for a consultant. While it is easier to get a decision made about something—simply ask the owner—where you go if you don't like the answer becomes a problem.

If your approach or recommendation is not immediately acceptable to the owner, you may be in trouble. Your first move, trying to convince him that you're right, may have slow going. This man is not used to people telling him he's wrong (even if you do it very well). To avoid telling him he's wrong, you may embark on a rather time-consuming process of trying to convince him that it was his idea in the first place. This negates the advantage of being able to get quick decisions from a single decision maker. Failing those approaches, your game is virtually over. There are often no other power sources in the company. You have no candidates for powerful individuals on your side of the discussion.

The notion of building countervailing forces in favor of or opposed to your position is fairly standard operating procedure in larger companies. It sometimes can work in smaller ones, if you choose your companies very carefully. It is not an automatic option in smaller companies, however, because owners are not managers. They see their stake in the company as total rather than as a job and, perhaps, some dividends from the equity.

But these problems are relatively minor when compared with the potential for real abuses of power. When the exercise of internal power begins to wash over into broader arenas, the owner—and those who try to work around him—may have difficulties. Some owners, for example, begin to believe that they can control anything and make everyone dance to their tunes. For consultants who work with them, this presents a knotty set of problems. These owners appear to think that you should be able to do anything, including make bricks without straw or transform base metals into gold, just because they said they wanted you to do so. Telling such an owner that it can't be done or can't be done within his time or money constraints is a very difficult task. Some of them will firmly believe to the end that you just didn't want to do the work or, worse, that there was some nefarious reason behind your not wanting to comply with their demands. I tend to avoid working with such owners—if I can spot them in time. You at least ought to be aware that they're out there. I discuss these areas at length in later chapters of the book. There are sections that may help you spot different varieties of owners and help you develop methods for addressing many of these difficulties.

It should be clear by now that working with smaller companies is really quite different from working with larger companies. I find the differences exciting and inherently interesting. Since you are reading this book, I assume that you also find smaller company potential interesting. The reason for considering these broad differences between smaller companies and others, however, is not pure intellectual enjoyment or sociological interest. It is good, hard business consideration. Smaller companies form the bulk of companies in the United States. While I cannot quote you a number (because, amazingly enough, nobody really knows how many companies there are or how one should define *small*), small companies form at least 90 percent of all companies. According to the Internal Revenue Service and the Small Business Administration, they produce the bulk of new jobs and most of the first jobs in the economy.

The numbers of smaller companies and the vitality of the small business sector as a whole make working with smaller companies plain good business. Once you figure out how to get in and what they need to buy from you, they are a great market. As is true of any market, however, you will not even get your foot in the door if you have no idea what you are dealing with. You will certainly not stay in this market if you cannot play the games that are unique to smaller companies.

This chapter began to show you some critical areas in which many business advice sources are too glib when it comes to smaller companies. In reading or listening to such material, when smaller companies are addressed at all, there is the underlying sense that everything is the same, only smaller. It is my contention that there are fundamental differences between larger and smaller companies. I further contend that if you are not aware of these differences and if you do not adapt your approaches and methods to the different reality, you will not do nearly as well in this segment as you could.

The broad general differences outlined here will affect your consulting practice to the extent that you choose to work with smaller companies. Some—differences relating to the role of the owner, for example—will significantly affect the process of selling consulting projects. Others, often those described under company differences, will significantly affect the consulting process you will follow. In short, your ability to be effective and to enjoy and profit from working with smaller companies depends, I believe, on your ability to recognize and work through these differences. Helping you to do so is the purpose of the remainder of this book.

2

HOW CONSULTANTS FIT IN SMALLER COMPANIES

The key fact to remember about consultants, particularly those operating in smaller company environments, is that they have no inherent power. This being the case, it is necessary for anyone wishing to be effective at providing real assistance to a smaller company to recognize potential sources of influence and to use them well. It is also wise to remain constantly aware of the limitations of the consulting role and to work to minimize them.

This chapter focuses on the role(s) of consultants in smaller companies. It considers sources and uses of power and influence for outsiders in smaller companies. With that perspective, it examines how and why you are there and some methods and approaches to doing the job that seem to work well across a broad spectrum of smaller companies. It assumes that your objective is to be effective: to influence some change or modification, to have some method or procedure or approach accepted and implemented. As you will see, a perfect way to undercut these aims is to presume a level of power you do not have.

A CAUTIONARY TALE

A consultant was sent by a bank into a smaller company. His mandate was to develop a control system that would permit the company to report results appropriately and often to managers and to the bank. The consultant believed that his bank backing would provide enough influence and impetus to carry him through the project. *Wrong!* It seems that the owner and the bank had been at odds over reporting practices since the original loan had been signed. The owner preferred to tell nothing to anybody. He insisted on the bare minimum of bank reporting and on offering no information whatever to his managers or staff.

Of course, the bank *should* have mentioned this minor issue to the consultant prior to sending him off to do battle with the owner. Alternatively, the consultant *should* have spent some of his initial time just listening and watching, determining what the issues really were. Since neither of these two things occurred, the consultant simply breezed into the company, assuming that the bank and the owner agreed about what needed to be done.

In short order, this consultant had his recommendation for hardware rejected ("Too expensive"), his recommendations on paper flow sidetracked ("Jack doesn't get his figures out before the fifth of the month"), and his report distribution proposals virtually ignored. After the consultant finished his process, the bank and the owner each had a copy of a report that would serve well as a doorstop. The bank remained frustrated. The owner exulted in another "victory" over the bank. The consultant went on to another project—but not for that bank or for that owner (or his acquaintances). The truly amazing thing was that he could not figure out what had gone wrong with this rather simple assignment.

SOURCES AND USES OF POWER/INFLUENCE

This consultant assumed he had a level of influence that he did not actually have. Thus, he acted in ways that did not permit him to develop any. While his task may have been impossible to achieve in any case, given the circumstances, his method of operation in the company guaranteed that the project would fail.

Unlike the situation in most large companies, there are usually few well-formed countervailing power groups in smaller companies. There also tend to be fewer outside relationships that can be used to build influence. Finally, relationships tend to be more personal and less subject to rational factors in smaller companies than in large companies. All these factors make it more difficult for an outsider—in this case, the consultant—to develop and nurture a strong base. And, for a consultant to be effective, a base has to be developed rapidly, within the project time frame.

The kinds and amounts of power and influence that are being considered here are not the kinds that conquer nations (necessarily). They permit a consultant to get a particular task accomplished efficiently and effectively. They cause owners, managers, and other personnel to listen and to give serious consideration to conclusions and recommendations. There are relatively few sources of such power and influence in any circumstance.

Money or ownership. This is the kind of power and influence that comes with owning the place and, theoretically, being able to "clean house" or shut the place down if the spirit moves you. Clearly, this power belongs to the owner(s) and is entirely unavailable to a consultant.

Position. This kind of power in a company ultimately stems from a person's ability to hire and fire. Depending on the nature of the particular project you are called on to perform, you, as consultant, may indirectly acquire some of this kind of power. If, for example, you are making recommendations about the reorganization of a function, you may hold jobs (and job content) in your hands.

Personal. In political circles, this is often referred to as "charisma." It is the ability to lead your troops through *anything* and have them glad to go. It is the ability to move people through personal magnetism. It is something you either have or you don't. It operates independent of the company you are in or the particular project you are doing. It must be a handy item for a consultant to have, since it is easily portable from project to project, but I am living proof that you do not have to have it to succeed in consulting.

Knowledge or expertise. This is the basis for most of the power and influence that consultants can develop. It is generally limited to the areas in which the particular consultant is recognized to have a level of knowledge that is respected. These limitations can be expanded through using some of the techniques discussed later, in Chapter 9. You should also be aware that the key word in this description is *recognized.* If your knowledge is not recognized and acknowledged, no influence can flow from it or its exercise.

While any kind of influence that helps get your job done should be acceptable, clearly the kind to strive for is the professionally based influence that derives from mastery of your subject matter. This kind of influence separates you from the insiders without building walls around you. It is possible to "grow" this kind of influence. It can be effective in numerous companies, while other kinds of power (except the personal kind) tend to be rooted in a specific company or consulting situation. In short, to succeed in this business, a prime consideration should be how to develop and use the influence and power stemming from your expertise (Chapters 4 and 5).

For the moment, however, consider the fact that many of the levels of your potential to influence a client company are set at the time you walk through the door. If, for example, you sign on for a certain kind of project, some position power may attach to you. If you sign on as an outsider (as did the consultant mentioned earlier), you will probably have access to little or no power. Given this situation, it becomes extremely important for a consultant to determine why the project is being done at all so she can assess the tools that will be available.

WHAT ARE YOU DOING THERE—REALLY?

Given the preceding discussion, this apparently silly question sounds only slightly less dumb. After all, you are a consultant. Your job is to work with client companies. You make money. The client gets his problems solved. End of issue. Right? Well, sometimes. . . .

As you will notice as we go along, determining the problem is often the key to getting the job done. And your first problem is determining why you really have been asked to come into a company or to talk seriously with its owners or managers. One way of dealing with this problem is simply to ignore it—assume you are there for the reasons they say you are there. You may even be right. The difficulty with this approach is that, if you are wrong, you may have blown the whole show before you even get started.

A better approach is not to trust to luck or to assumption. As a consultant, your first question should always be what you are really supposed to be doing wherever you are working. The initial answer is usually very simple. The bank's consultant was there to develop an information system. Very straightforward and fairly standard, as assignments go. As noted, the simple answer may be the real answer—but don't count on it.

Especially in a smaller company, the second-level answer is what you need even before you decide to take on the project. While the true purpose of a project should be a question for all consultants in all companies, it tends to be a more critical problem for those of us who deal with smaller companies. This is because of two differences described in Chapter 1 between smaller and larger companies.

First, the power structure is smaller and less complex in smaller companies. In real life, this means that there are fewer sources of power and influence. It is thus less possible to develop effective countervailing opinions about what really needs to be done. Second, because smaller companies are so often one- or two-man shows, it is easier to derail a project there than in a larger company. In a smaller company, you are generally dealing directly with those who hold the only power to make changes directly. If they become convinced—through even a chance remark—that you have the purpose wrong, you are through. There is less opportunity to correct than there may be in a larger company with a layered power structure. And once you have been written off by those in total control, the project is most likely dead—whether or not they let you finish it.

Thus, as you can see, figuring out why you are there is important. Both the actual purpose and your response to it are likely to affect both your performance and the probability of project success. Incidentally, this issue is also likely to affect your probability of getting paid for your effort. Owners of smaller companies are notorious for refusing to pay for something they did not receive (a reasonable position, on the whole). Answering the wrong question makes them fairly certain they did not receive what they bargained for.

POTENTIAL UNDERLYING REASONS FOR BEING THERE

With these potential consequences of incorrect assumptions or judgments firmly in mind, this section considers some of the real reasons that you might have been invited into a smaller company. As you will see, some of them are clearly legitimate purposes; that is, they will accord with your notions of what you should be doing in the consulting business. Some are less clearly OK. Others might cause you to decide that you don't want to take on the work. (I discuss *your* objectives later in this chapter.)

The key notion is that you will not be able to give your client a truly satisfactory answer until you know what prompted the question. Part of this discussion of broad potential purposes considers how specific kinds of failures to understand can affect the dynamics of a project.

Clearly Legitimate Reasons for Working with a Consultant

Expertise.   Most consultants tend to assume that the owner or manager is calling on outside skills and talents because they are unavailable inside the company. This is certainly the most personally flattering reason that a consultant can encounter. Being invited in for this reason confers a measure of instant knowledge-based power. This assumption generally includes the notion that you, as consultant, will also be teacher, mentor, and guru all rolled into one—and you will even get paid for basking in all this respect and adulation!

The key assumptions in this scenario are that you have *and the client recognizes* a high level of specific expertise, that your expertise conveys a certain measure of power and influence (at least within the realm of your particular subject), and that the client is willing and eager to learn from you. When this is the true reason, you have a project that is a joy to work on. All you have to do is your own thing to your usual excellent standard of performance. People listen. Recommendations are implemented. You are likely to get follow-on work from this client and referrals to other owners and/or managers. Assuming you really are expert, you can't lose.

But consider what occurs if you make these assumptions and expertise is *not* the real reason you are there. You appear (and perhaps are) arrogant. You assume that influence stemming from your expertise is at your disposal when it is not. You try to use it and you turn people off. You teach when nobody particularly wants to learn. In short, you come off very badly. More to the point, people stop listening and the project (whatever the work actually was) suffers.

So, flattering though it may be, always consider carefully the assumption that you are there solely or largely because of your expertise. If the assumption is incorrect, you risk disaster. If, on the other hand, you assume that other factors may well account for your presence in that company, you are unlikely to do yourself or your project any harm. This last does *not* mean that you should discount your expertise or retain less confidence in your skills and abilities—they are, in fact, what you sell—but that you should not assume that your client either holds them in the same esteem you do or really recognizes them at all. What he or she needs from you may be something entirely different. It is part of your job to find out.

Extra hands and/or bodies.   Some consultants refer to this purpose as "body-shopping"—with a sniff of distaste. However, one of the key facts about smaller companies is that they are small. They lack the hot-and-cold-running staff of their larger cousins. Quite often an owner or manager wants to perform a specific project for which there is simply not enough free time among existing personnel. The only way for her to get it done is to go outside for the people. Unless the need is for clerical or secretarial staff, a standard temporary agency simply will not do. You and your group are elected.

This situation most often occurs for one of two reasons. Either the company is trying to decide whether a certain course of action makes sense for the longer term (at which point they will hire the necessary bodies full time) or the company simply has a short-term crunch of some sort. This can be a peak that pulls current employees off ongoing work (which your group will take care of for the interim), or it can be a new short-term project for which the owner/manager believes full-time staffing would be wasteful. Your group then takes care of the specific project. The specifics are often less clear than they appear here.

In *some* of these situations, your expertise in a particular field may well be called on. For example, if you are staffing a new short-term project, you may also be required to teach the methods you develop. If the company is in a feasibility phase (whether they call it that or not), your input into the value of the project/line of business/whatever, may be sought. *But that is not your primary purpose in being there.* You are really there to get the work out. You are probably being paid for bodies, not advice. (*Note:* These projects are fertile grounds for discovering what a company really needs by way of expertise consulting, however. Use them well, but don't push.)

A variant on body-shopping that is growing rapidly in today's small business environment combines the provision of personnel with some expertise consulting. In general, the cost squeeze on smaller companies has made many owners rethink the notion that they need full staffs to cover all company functions. They are particularly unwilling to invest in full-time help that is likely to cost a great deal and be only partly utilized in the company—an eminently reasonable position. The solution is increasingly becoming the use, on a continuing basis, of an outside, specialized, professional group. This group essentially takes over the responsibility for the specified function, serving almost (but not quite) as part-time employees.

This arrangement gives the owner functional flexibility at a higher level than would be possible if the function were in-house. It offers the outside professionals a continuing arrangement and source of fees—known in the trade as an *annuity*—presumably forever. Or at least until the company grows to such a size where it can support a highly professional in-house version of that function. (You will then, probably, get to help the owner decide who and what is really required in this replacement department.)

Not surprisingly, your position in the company under such an arrangement gives you a great deal of flexibility and, perhaps, even more power (influence) than a standard consulting role. You are likely to be there for the long term. Therefore, you become a force to be reckoned with rather than someone who is just there for a project. Moreover, a continuing record of good work and advice confirms your expertise and value and makes further influence within the company likely. You become somewhat like insiders, but with a greater independence and, probably, a louder voice.

There are drawbacks, however, to this outsider/insider role for a consultant. The owner may, for example, begin to think of you and act toward you as if you were really an employee. If you accept such treatment, you seriously undermine both your true value to your client and your potential for future consulting work with that client. In effect, you cease being a consultant and begin being a temporary agency. If that is your objective, it's fine. If, however, you wish to continue being a consultant, you need to catch and correct such behavior early. The key is being aware that it is beginning.

Consulting in this hybrid form seems to be making the greatest inroads in the personnel and financial areas. It seems clear that owners frequently believe that their companies can get along with outsiders in these positions. Alternatively, they may believe that such functions are so complex and/or critical that hiring adequate personnel in-house would be prohibitively expensive. In either case, if you operate in one of these fields, you might consider whether this is the sort of business you want to do. If you are in some other areas and find these arrangements attractive, you might consider whether your field offers any opportunity for developing similar long-term client relationships.

The hot potato.   Essentially, assignments in this genre really do not require your expertise. Everyone knows the answer to the problem. The issue is who is going to take the heat for a solution that some (all?) of the people in the company will not like one bit. If you take the job, you're it.

This is one of those "iffy" areas of a consulting practice. You are walking into a situation in which you are expected to come up with an "answer" that is known (decided?) in advance. While this is generally *not* considered a legitimate purpose for a consultant, often the situation really *is* clearcut. The "answer" really *is* the answer. In fact, the problem that you are handling for the owner or manager is not the issue at all. It is the *consequence* of the answer that is the problem. The time frame and cost that the client expects will, of course, be commensurate with the problem he really wants solved.

Such assignments are generally rather easy, if you have a thick skin. You are walking in knowing that you will not be loved when you walk out. This is, of course, a serious consideration, both professionally and personally, in deciding whether to take on the project. Consider a situation in which some of your prospective client's people are quite likely to be in consultant-hiring positions in other companies in the relatively near future. You might deem it detrimental to your business to take on an assignment in which you *know* they are going to be distressed with you. In some industries or areas, reputations get around so rapidly that you may want to think twice about taking on such hot potatoes.

The consequences of misunderstanding the client's true reason for calling you can be serious here as well. Suppose, for example, the request for a proposal from you is phrased as, say, a study of two alternative approaches to an employee benefit plan. What is really wanted is an outsider to recommend strongly that the company adopt the alternative that is financially more beneficial to the company but less beneficial to the employees. You will also be expected to discuss or develop implementation plans. Proposing a full-blown study will likely put you out of the running on cost grounds alone. Confirmation generally costs less and takes less elapsed time.

This discussion of hot potatoes assumes that the answer that "everyone knows" is really the right answer (to the right problem). If what the client really wants is your agreement with a solution or a problem assessment that is not so clearcut, you may have a serious decision to make. This situation is discussed further in the next section.

Not-So-Legitimate Reasons for Calling a Consultant

As you will see, some of the less legitimate reasons for which owners and managers call consultants are rather close to some of the perfectly legitimate ones. In addition, the less legitimate reasons are similar to one another in the sense that the consultant becomes part of a game in which the actual project or piece of work that was contracted generally has little to do with why the consultant is really there. The lines among the various types are often indistinct and those between the legitimate and not-so-legitimate are so blurry at times that one hesitates to recommend a course of action to a consultant without examining the specific situation. The list of general areas that follows is intended to alert you to what your potential client may really be asking for—before you cheerfully contract to give it to her.

Pawn in a long-term war. This is the trap into which our friend the consultant sent by the bank so blithely fell. He was essentially a single salvo in a continuing battle. Such battles occur, of course, in companies of all sizes. As such, they represent hazards to all consultants. But, as you will see, there are fewer ways to find out what is really going on in a smaller company. There are likely to be, for example, fewer bystanders or nonparticipants who can give you a somewhat less biased viewpoint.

The battle or plot is likely to be clearer and more blatant in a smaller company, however. Some of the more common plots are almost soap opera material. There's the one about the son taking over control of the business from his father. Then, there's the one about the warring partners who haven't spoken to each other directly in thirty years. Actually, there are probably about as few standard plots in smaller company internal wars as there are truly different plots for novels. Knowing this, however, will not help you to perform whatever task you agreed to do should you inadvertently end up in the middle of one of them.

The trick is to recognize that there is a game going on that your prospective project figures in somehow. You then must evaluate, *in the context of that particular game*, your potential for successfully completing whatever piece of work you are considering *before* you commit to doing it. In determining whether you even want to try to do that particular piece of work, you might also remember that if you are part of the battle, your success will distress at least one of the warring factions. When you win, somebody loses. In the earlier story, the consultant lost, the owner won, and the bank lost. The project did not really matter—except in terms of the ongoing war.

Concurring in a predetermined solution. This is perhaps the most difficult to differentiate from the hot potato project. In both cases, the answer is known before the consultant walks in. The major underlying issues are what is backing the answer and what the consultant is supposed to do.

In a hot potato situation, there is generally a significant amount of work, writing, and thought behind the conclusion that you are supposed to support. The assumption on the part of the owners/ managers who brought you in, in fact, is that, had you done all the work yourself, you would have reached the same conclusions. More to the point, when you see what they have already done, you will approve. You, as the consultant, are also supposed to *do* something (generally regarding implementation or implementation planning) for which you will take the heat.

In a concurrence situation, in contrast, you are likely to find little by way of solid documentation behind the predetermined answer. Often, in fact, your project is defined as finding the data and/ or rationales to support the predetermined answer. Data to the contrary will be unacceptable—however valid and authoritative. Moreover, you are generally not asked to *do* anything other than to dig up support. You merely add your voice to that of the person who brought you in.

The problem here lies in the possibility that you might assume that you have been asked to find an answer rather than to document an already chosen response. Should you make that assumption—and happen to reach the wrong conclusion—you are quite likely not to get paid for your time, effort, and expertise. The client is seeking to buy your support, using your reputation for expertise while refusing to let you exercise it.

When considering doing this kind of project, keep in mind that your reputation (which is why the client wants *your* support) will not withstand your uncritical support of too many predetermined conclusions. Nobody's can.

Study as a substitute for doing anything.   As you have probably already noticed, sometimes the best way of doing absolutely nothing is in a flurry of activity. Consultants can help create a very effective and pretty flurry of activity. Happily, because of the expense and general disruption of having a flurry-creating project done by consultants, this particular kind of nonproject tends to afflict larger companies to a greater extent than smaller ones. There isn't enough money and most owners hold enough power on their own to do just plain nothing if they feel like it.

Such nonprojects do appear from time to time, however, typically as part of a larger battle between an outside force and the owner. Such battles might arise between owner and bank, money partner and working partners, or minority shareholders or board members and the owner/managers. The same ideas apply as those discussed previously under "Wars." Had our friend the bank's consultant not gotten into the battle directly, he might have had a study that was really a nonproject. (In fact, had he noticed that he had inadvertently gotten into the middle of a war, that might have been his best strategy. He could have delivered his report and left the bank and the owner to fight it out themselves.)

WARNING SIGNALS

A critical issue is how you know when you are about to walk into a not-so-legitimate situation or to differentiate among the reasons that might have brought you into this owner/manager's office. The keys, as is true in most consulting situations, are listening and watching.

As mentioned earlier, figuring out what you are really supposed to be doing may be easier in a smaller company than in a large one.

The owner/manager who asks you in may be fairly blatant about what she really wants. The general feeling is often that whatever she wants, she can buy. Holding (almost) absolute power through ownership and money sometimes becomes a habit of mind. If what she seeks from you is something you believe is unethical, improper, or against your best business interest, saying so may not be easy. In these cases, while your task of figuring may be easier, your decision regarding how to handle the situation may be less so.

More likely, the signals that you are being asked to do something that may not be totally legitimate are fairly subtle. If the real reason for your presence is some internecine war, you may be told that you should not (or may not) talk with Jack Johnson, the manager of a department that may be affected by the project. While a list of reasons may be supplied for omitting Jack from your list of interviewees, there are quite likely to be too many good reasons. They will begin to sound to your ears like justifications—if you are listening between the lines. There may be really good reasons. You have to listen carefully and judge whether you are about to get into the middle of some power game or whether the project will really be better off if you skip old Jack.

If you are really being asked to concur in a decision already made, you will, if you listen carefully, most likely hear statements that assume the answer to the question that you are being asked to investigate. The person with whom you are talking is telling you the answer. Try pointing out (nonjudgmentally) that he has made an assumption about the result. If you get a strange or surprised look, you are probably being faced with a demand for concurrence. Alternatively, you may get a conspiratorial grin in response. Should that occur, you know that the speaker is more convinced that you are going to do what he really wants. What you do from there is up to you.

In short, through listening and watching the people who are bringing you into a company, you can usually get a good idea about what the job really is. You then must decide what to do about it.

YOUR OBJECTIVES

Which brings us, of course, to a section on what your objectives might be as a consultant (in any of its forms) to a smaller company. My purpose here is not to make ethical or moral judgments but rather to outline a number of objectives that you can examine, see which (if any) fit, and modify as you wish. I have tried, in this section more than most others, to be dispassionate and to identify my personal and professional beliefs where relevant. To the extent that I fail and sound judgmental, I apologize in advance.

My objective in this section is to ask you to think about why you are doing what you are doing. While doing so will help you to build a coherent practice, it will also assist you in sorting through the ethical issues that were touched on in the last section. If you have a clear understanding of your objectives in taking on a client project, and a priority among them, deciding which jobs to accept and which to reject on ethical grounds will be a great deal easier for you. To place this discussion squarely in this context, this section discusses only potential objectives vis-à-vis client projects.

The first issue that generally comes up in discussing the objectives of a consultant, or anyone in independent business, is money. However much you love the process of consulting and the results, etc., you also need to eat. Making money, therefore, is undoubtedly somewhere on your list of objectives for a consulting project and for any given client. It is quite reasonable for you to wish (demand, if necessary) to get paid for your skill, expertise, whatever it is you are selling to clients. The question with which you need to begin to deal is how much of which other objectives you are prepared to compromise to get how much money.

While outright propositions that you perform in certain ways for a given amount of money are relatively rare, some of the client objectives described in "Not-So-Legitimate Reasons" are really only prettified versions of the same thing. When you determine your own objectives in handling client projects, you will see more clearly the damage you might do by taking on a project that *you* consider (or others might consider) not legitimate or ethical.

Essentially, part of your job is making trade-offs between the requirements of jobs and clients and your requirements of yourself and your practice. Were you working for a company, your boss or a policy manual could serve as a model for "what is done here." As an independent consultant, you are all there is; you must develop your own model. The following possible objectives for client projects might get you thinking in helpful ways.

Being Efficient at Getting the Client's Project Done

This objective is in obvious opposition to your desire to make money in client projects. Unless you are operating in a fixed price environment, more time spent on a project means more money to you. The dangers in choosing to maximize time rather than efficiency lie in consistently exceeding your estimates of time and cost and in the possibility that the owner/manager for whom you are doing the project may know approximately how long the work *should* take. The word does get around.

Being Effective at Getting the Client's Project Done

This may require some compromise with your personal preferences and, sometimes, with the efficiency objective. It may mean, for example, letting someone in the client organization whom you really dislike take credit for your work. It may mean having more meetings than you would like to create consensus on issues critical to the project. In some of these situations, it may help to remember that even if your credit is not public, some people in the client company know what you have done (and what they paid serious money to have you do). That word also gets around.

Seeing To It That the Client Gets What Is Needed

This is not necessarily the same thing as giving the client what she wants. You, as the professional, may believe that part of your role is to try to get your client to see what is really needed—even if that is not what you were brought in to do.

I have turned down projects in which I could not shift the prospective client from where he started to what he should be looking at. This is not pure altruism. If you do a project that should not be done at all simply for the money, you run two risks. First, sometime the client may see that the wrong problem is being addressed and hold you responsible. "I told you so" will not be considered an adequate response. Second, even if the client never sees the real problem that you targeted, your project will not solve the problem he saw. He will, therefore, be dissatisfied with your work. In short, this is a game you cannot win in the longer run.

Setting Clients Up to Do It Themselves Next Time

A key notion in my small company consulting practice is that the client should have to call a consultant only once for a given type of problem. For me, this is a strategy issue and is discussed further in Chapter 10. The issue for any consultant, however, is the conflict between money (in the form of repeat business) and efficiency and effectiveness. Clearly, if you enable the client to operate more on her own, you lose the opportunity to do the same job again for that client later. A real question is whether you would be bored doing the same things over and over. A more substantive question lies in your view of the role of a consultant in a smaller company. Is your role only to do the particular project? Or is it closer to the role of a teacher/mentor to smaller companies? (In general, I have found that there are enough new problems to require repeat business. And I don't get bored with my work.)

Maintaining Personal Integrity

This one can be short and sweet. If maintaining personal integrity is of primary importance to you, the first issue in considering a project is whether you would feel right about doing the proposed piece of work. If you wouldn't, don't. This may, obviously, conflict with your desire to make money, but if you find yourself trying to design loopholes in your conscience as you are listening to a potential client describe a project, skip it. You are unlikely to find loopholes. You will be ambivalent about the project and, therefore, unlikely to do a great job anyway. Most important for your long-run mental health, you will begin to have second thoughts about yourself. I cannot think of anything that would be worth that.

Maintaining and Enhancing Professional Reputation

This, as a project purpose, tends to include more than simply doing a great job for a client. It usually also implies a need to publicize that great job. Such a situation may occur as you extend your specialty field or move into a new geographic area. This may raise ethical issues since many clients, particularly small company clients, are absolutely rabid about the notion that you might disclose anything about their companies to anyone outside. Some may even feel that the very act of calling for assistance is a personal failure. They may not permit you to mention their names as clients. If you consider this matter rationally, you will see that this is their right, however irrational it may seem to you. If your sole purpose in taking on that particular project, then, is reputation building, you will need to find a more congenial client for whom to do similar work.

If, alternatively, your purpose is simply to maintain your reputation or to get good press from the client, you can do that quite easily with any client except those who will not admit they actually called a consultant. Assuming you do well for them, they are likely to talk about you with their peers. If you did an outstanding job, however, giving the company some competitive edge, you can bet that those peers will not include competitors. (You might also consider your policies about doing similar projects for competitors.)

SO HOW *DO* CONSULTANTS FIT?

The ambiguous, but direct, answer to the question is: "However they agree to fit." It is not definitive but, in consulting, few things are.

As you can see from the broad range of possible purposes of each party in a consulting transaction, consultants can have a place in smaller company operations. The key is that there must be a good fit between the purpose(s) of the client in seeking assistance and the purpose(s) of the consultant offering it. Whether the match will work out well in practice for both parties depends, in addition, on the skills and abilities of both parties, but particularly those of the consultant, the outsider. She is, after all, the professional.

Part II

CONSULTING TO SMALLER COMPANIES

3

THE CONSULTING RELATIONSHIP: DEVELOPING SALES

Consulting, to smaller companies in particular, is based largely on relationships. While it is true that *all* consulting is personal to some extent, in a smaller company everything tends to be more personal than it is in a larger company. The owner(s) and/or manager(s) tend to know the employees personally. Personal tastes and predilections tend to be more controlling.

This situation is only partly a function of sheer size. It is often a matter of company policy or a function of the personality of the owner. Old family companies, for example, often take pride in the personal relationship between owners (family members) and employees. Newer entrepreneurial firms may not yet have reached the stage at which management of the company becomes more "professional" and detached—that is, less personal. These firms may still be in the stage where the owner makes all the decisions and believes she can (should?) operate with personal factors playing a significant role.

While there is a great deal of research on the personal styles of entrepreneurs and owners of family companies, the purpose here is not a general survey of the literature or a detached discussion of an interesting phenomenon. The main purpose of raising the issue is to consider the impact of those styles, and of size in general, on the problems of providing consulting services to such companies. And they do often raise issues for professional consultants.

As you will see, the personal/company styles of the people with whom you will be doing business affect the way contacts and sales are made. They affect how image and expertise are viewed and certified. They affect the kinds of arrangements that consultants are likely to be able to make with their smaller company clients. They affect follow-on work and referrals. In short, the entire consulting relationship may be affected by differences in personal and management styles of smaller companies.

This being the case, the chapter also considers how best to adjust generally recommended consulting tactics to accommodate these styles. In general, you will notice that the consulting process does not change. The changes are largely attitudinal. Nevertheless, they are critical to succeeding at management consulting to smaller companies.

MAKING CONTACT

Owners of smaller companies tend to be locally oriented. More to the point, they tend to prefer working with people they know and trust—preferably people with whom they have worked before. For a would-be consultant to such a company, then, the issue is how to achieve the status of one known and trusted by area/regional small company owners.

Joining Up

One answer to the question of how to become known by area business owners is the same as that given to all consultants: Go where they are. But from there, your answer diverges, largely because where *your* targets are differs from where their targets are in more ways than one. While large company executives tend to join functionally oriented groups (associations of training executives or personnel groups, for example), professional societies, and various social clubs, owners of smaller companies tend to join area or regional associations designed especially for smaller company owners. Since you run a small company (your consulting business), you may be eligible to join also.

But joining and sitting in the back of the room during meetings and presentations will do you little professional good—even if you circulate and hand out lots of business cards. To your potential clients you will be simply another name on the membership list. In addition to joining, you need to become active, to become known in the organization. Given the thin staffing and general hunger for workers, speakers, writers, etc., the easiest way is to offer to help.

How you do this should depend on your own skills and areas of expertise. In general, however, it should not be done the first time you show up. You will need time to consider the structure of the group, whether there are any special interest subgroups that might meet your needs better than the group as a whole, who shows up at meetings, and so on. Once you have a good sense of how the organization operates (and who its leaders are), make a targeted offer.

Suppose, for example, you attend a program, the format of which might lend itself to a discussion of an area of your expertise. You believe that the topic would be something of general interest to the group. Of course, it will also be in an area in which you offer consulting services. You might try specifically offering to present a similar program. The offer must be as professional as your presentation will be. Your proposed program will need a catchy title, and the proposal must provide enough of an outline to show the program committee that you will be offering useful information and not just selling your consulting services. You will find—if you haven't already done so—that people, small company owners in particular, are wary of consultants selling at them.

If your specific offer is accepted, your debut before the group is as an expert in your consulting field. You will, of course, mention your business (or have it mentioned for you) in your introduction. But that is the last time you should mention it. Present information that is useful. Demonstrate your expertise. When answering questions, you can use such phrases as "In my experience" or "In such situations I have found." But go no further. Your business will have been noted. You will be well regarded for not "making a pitch" on their time.

Given what was said earlier about the preference of owners to work with those they have worked with before, however, you will probably want to go beyond making presentations to the group. You might actually want to work with the organization itself. It would probably be very helpful, for example, to join the membership committee. You would then get to work with current members in recruiting and welcoming new members. In short, there is probably a lot to do, and it is likely to be worth some of your time to do it.

Even if (or when) you are not directly working with a group, you can become known in it. You simply play consultant/teacher in a low-key way at regular presentations. Sticking closely to your area(s) of expertise, you simply raise questions of other speakers or group members. This must be done very carefully so you don't offend either the speakers or the group. Speakers do not come with backup plans for audience harassment. Most audiences at that kind of affair react negatively to verbal contests or highly aggressive behavior.

Frame your questions to invite useful extensions or elaborations. You might preface the question with a brief allusion to your practice/experience: "In my work, I have found that many. . . . How do you suggest that owners/managers handle . . . ?" While this approach is not a real alternative for speaking in the first instance, it can offer a start to being viewed within the organization as someone who knows something. And asking the right questions is always good practice for a consultant.

Taking Your Show on the Road

Another approach to becoming known in the area smaller business community is to perform other speaking/writing tasks. Some areas, for example, have local access cable television stations that are often looking for inexpensive programming that would be of interest to their audiences. If there is a local business-oriented show, so much the better. If you do not like to speak, or if there is no appropriate outlet, consider the local papers. Some areas have small business-oriented newspapers or discrete sections of larger newspapers. An offer to provide an occasional or regular column (with byline, of course) may produce your vehicle.

In all these situations, your choice of topic(s) is critical. Your audience will reach beyond those you consider true potential clients. Your work must reach the potential clients while also addressing the rest of the audience (or you won't have that forum for long). The key to success at topic choosing is to think the way you expect a generalist would and to focus on the broader issues that touch on whatever your special area is.

If, for example, your practice is in building custom software for smaller companies in the retail field, your speech/article might discuss the dangers of computerizing smaller companies. You can even make it wryly funny, if your style tends to that sort of humor. Discuss some of the odd cases you know, but take care not to appear to be laughing (or even smirking) at the poor unfortunate owners who got caught in the messes you are describing.

Properly packaged, a speech or article like this will play to *anyone* who thinks the current rush to computerize is overdone. Your piece will play particularly well to owners of smaller companies who have been resisting computerization. It will tell them not only that they are not crazy or hopelessly out of date but it will also tell them, subtly, that they can get the benefits of computerization without the headaches—if they work with someone who knows the pitfalls (you).

Your purpose here is not making money with your speaking/ writing, although you might, in fact, be paid (in tiny sums) for some of it. Your purpose is becoming recognized in your area among potential clients for your services. Consider the time and effort as part of your business development effort. And never lose sight of why you are really doing whatever you are doing.

Political Involvement

Another good meeting ground for consultants seeking small company clients is the political arena. This does not mean that you need to consider running for office or becoming active in local party politics (unless, of course, that is your thing anyway). It does mean that you should become aware of the major issues in your local area, assessing them for the potential application of your area(s) of expertise.

Local issues tend to matter more to owners/managers of smaller companies than to industry giants. This makes sense since the average owner/manager has one plant or store in one location. Anything that affects that particular operation has impact on his entire business. Moreover, an owner of a smaller company does not have enough clout alone to affect the outcome. The effects of most local actions on the total well-being of a national or multinational company, by contrast, are likely to be relatively minimal. Thus, owners of local small companies are likely to be vitally interested in the political activities that could affect the firm. Your (disinterested) participation and support are likely to be noted and appreciated.

Naturally you will not want to contravene your most cherished political principles for the sake of mere business. (If you try to do that, you are likely to appear insincere and actually be ineffective anyway.)

But once you have studied the issues, should you reach conclusions favorable to your potential clientele, why not make your views public? Such forums as city councils, zoning boards, and their ilk tend to get a great deal of local press, and that can be good business for you.

BUILDING CONFIDENCE AMONG POTENTIAL CLIENTS

Once you have met your potential clients in nonselling settings, your next task is to convince them—without appearing to do so—that you are loyal, trustworthy, and responsible, in addition to being good at what you do. Here, you are working against long-established prejudices against consultants in general.

I recall sitting across the desk once from a very reluctant potential client. As we worked through his rational objections, it became clear that something else was going on in the meeting. Eventually, it came out. The last consultant with whom this president had worked had taken him for one heck of a ride. For $40,000 (in 1976), this consultant had presented him with the same report that had been given to at least three other owners. Only the names had been changed. Even some critical details had been left as they were, despite their irrelevance to this specific company. Without a history of contact with this particular president, there was no way I was going to sell what I came to sell. Even referrals would have been unlikely to work, since the previous "consultant" had been recommended by supposedly responsible colleagues.

While you may not run across numerous potential clients who have been thus burned, almost everyone has heard the horror stories. There are a lot of unscrupulous folks out there. Without a confidence-building phase, your potential client may simply assume that you are quite likely to be just another consultant out to make a buck at her expense. (I have assumed that she would not be right.)

What Sells?

This, of course, is the key question. This section skips the standard consulting book advice about such things as neat proposals and dressing appropriately for what you seek to do. It assumes that either you have already figured that out or you can read it elsewhere. What this section discusses, rather, are attributes you have or can build that will inspire the confidence of your potential clients. It stresses that what really sells is not selling at all, but rather a real and basic underlying concern for the difficulties of the people with whom you work or wish to work.

Your task is to build confidence in two separate areas: professional and personal. On a professional level, you must inspire confidence in the value (innovativeness, speed, daring, whatever) of your work. On a more personal level, your potential client will have to trust you before he will permit you real access to his company. Your reputation counts in both instances, as do any associations you may have had—even indirectly or briefly—with the potential client.

In the professional arena, you will have already made a good start if you have been writing and speaking regularly on issues relevant to your consulting expertise. Keep in mind, however, that most owners of smaller companies are relentlessly pragmatic. They are interested in what works rather than the latest, most elegant theory about what ought to work. While a scholarly paper in a respected journal might draw respect, the overriding interest is more likely to be in a nuts-and-bolts how-to article on an area of special difficulty for them.

In fact, it is possible that a reputation for scholarly work may turn some potential clients away from you. The concern might be for your practicality—liberally mixed with some concern about being able to understand you and/or appearing or feeling stupid. Whatever else you may do by way of writing or speaking, however, if you can gain a reputation for being able to explain complexity in reasonable terms, you will do well working with smaller company clients.

On the personal front, the keys are dependability and concern. If you have been working with your potential clients in various community or association projects, they will already know that you do what you say you will. The particular work you take on in these groups can demonstrate your general concern for smaller companies and their owners/managers.

But even these contacts will rarely cement a relationship of trust. When you begin to talk with a single owner about her specific issues, you will need to provide other assurances, assurances that must be both clear and subtle. They are likely to take two main forms. First, you must assure your potential client that you mean what you say. Second, you must reaffirm a specific concern for her specific issues or problems.

Unfortunately, there is only one way to demonstrate that you mean what you say and that is to follow through. If you promise to deliver something—even something as essentially insignificant as this month's newsletter—to a potential client on a particular day, do it and do it *then*. The next day will not do. Until you have a fairly long association with your client, even one slip in this area can create unnecessary difficulties for you. Convincing someone that you are really not unreliable is a virtually impossible task.

The second part, demonstrating real concern about specific issues, tends to get consultants into a great deal of trouble. The problem is that the only way to achieve trust through such demonstrations is to listen and to respond. The obvious issue for you is: "How much response is reasonable?" You have to tread the thin line between being there for your potential client and giving away the store. Essentially, you are giving away some of your expertise for nothing. Some potential "clients" will take you for all they can get—as long as the price is right.

Unfortunately, there is no handy-dandy way to tell how much is enough. Over a period, you will begin to develop a sense of what feels right to you. The nonclient client sounds slightly grasping as he asks your advice when you meet. You find yourself going to some out-of-the-way city to see potential clients who know how far you have come to see them, yet the meeting does not move your consulting relationship any farther. My personal preference is to to err slightly on the side of giving away too much rather than not responding well enough, but that is really a personal choice.

How you end a relationship of that sort is also of concern. While you want "out," you do not want to leave a seriously disgruntled member of all the groups in town wandering around talking about your abrasiveness or failure to help. A method that tends to work reasonably well is to write a formal(ish) proposal to the potential client, outlining your response to the issues that have been raised, the specific work you propose to do, the time frame in which you propose to operate, the expected results of your program, and of course, the estimated cost of your proposed assistance. This approach is a clear statement to the effect that you sell advice for a living and that you would be pleased to do so for this company. While this may bring only a request that you elaborate on your proposed methods (tell them how to do it themselves), there will generally be good grounds, assuming your proposal is complete, on which to decline to do so. If you continue to ask them to sign, they will probably disappear in short order.

Whose Recommendation Counts?

You can sometimes short circuit a great deal of this reputation- and confidence-building process through the simple expedient of being recommended to the potential client in the right way by the right people. As is reasonable given the personal nature of much of the smaller-company ethic, a great deal of business is passed along in this manner. The trick is to get on the right grapevines.

Aside from relatives, friends, and trusted colleagues of specific owners of smaller companies, studies have shown that owners have the greatest amount of faith and trust in their accountants (see Table 3–1). Other outside professionals rank a bit behind. Consultants and college professors rank below the midpoint of the list. This tells you where your long-term development efforts must be targeted to have an impact on the small company community.

Clearly, you want to become known and trusted by the rest of the professional community in your area. Depending on your consulting specialties, your specific contact groups will be different. For example, one of my major consulting fields is management control and information methods—with or without computer systems. My

TABLE 3.1   Who Do They Trust?

Potential Advisor	Rank
Accountants, lawyers, etc.	1
Customers	2
Other small business owners	3
Business magazines	4
Trade associations	5
Bankers	6
Suppliers	7
Consultants	8
Colleges and universities	9
Chamber of commerce	10
Big firm business executives	11
Small Business Administration	12

Source: W. F. Kiesner, "Who Does the Small Business Owner Trust?," *Proceedings*, International Council for Small Business, October 1985.

best bets for developing a referral pattern within a professional community in this area would be through accountants and lawyers.

Accountants would be likely to see the need for my services most clearly and would also tend to be the professional an owner would ask first about services in this field. I would need to convince the accountants that I was not a competitor but would follow up on their bases, making their jobs easier. Because of the faith factor, lawyers are also often asked for advice about general business matters. My first task with area lawyers would be to help them to see the benefits that could be derived by a smaller company from using my services. Bankers would probably be the third group on my list. Although they would be a logical first or second choice given the nature of the specific consulting area, they rank lower because their referrals (according to surveys) rank lower with small company owners.

The process for establishing relationships with area professionals is similar to that for establishing any business relationships. You need to determine which individuals or firms might find your services particularly useful to know about. These are unlikely to be the largest firms in town. They are more likely to be solo practitioners or smaller firms very much like yours. You will probably be meeting them at the same places you have been meeting your potential clients. Do not be surprised when they expect you to get to know their specialty areas and to send recommendations their way as well.

This poses a bit of potential difficulty for you as a professional consultant. When you refer, your reputation goes on the line along with that of whomever you referred. This behooves you to check carefully the reputations (and, to the extent possible, the work) of the professionals with whom you choose to develop ties, however informal. Keep in mind also that these professionals are likely to be referring their own clients. Another factor in your choices, then, should be whether you are likely to work well with a particular professional or firm. Since these relationships are expected to be two-way streets, you should also do your best to make it easy for your potential referrers to build faith in the value of your work and the responsibility and concern of your services.

The process for creating this situation is slightly different from that discussed earlier for use with potential clients. The scholarly articles and your theoretical soundness are likely to make greater impressions in this arena than they will in the broader small business community. Since they know their clients and other potential referrals, however, they will also be considering your ability to work in the relevant companies along the lines discussed earlier.

Building such relationships involves not only getting to know the business interests and specialty areas of your various professional contacts but also supporting those areas. This part of your job need not be difficult or time consuming. It simply requires consideration and thought as you do whatever you normally do. For example, as I read publications or papers in my fields of interest, I am alert to their possible implications for my professional counterparts. When warranted, I send along a piece with a brief comment. This accomplishes three ends at once. First, it lets them know that I keep up with the relevant material in my field. Second, it tells them that I am concerned about their interests. Finally, it helps make a new connection between their businesses and my business. These three points help to develop a real professional relationship between the parties.

Developing relationships with bankers may be somewhat more difficult, given the groups you have joined. Bankers tend more toward the Chamber of Commerce/larger company model. The president of the largest bank in town, however, is not likely to be the person you need anyway. Many larger banks in cities or regions now have special small company lending groups. *These* are the bankers you want to get to know—and make sure they know you.

Bankers may be important in spotting potential users of your services among their clients. They are generally in a preferred position to know who needs what kind of assistance. However, bankers are often viewed by owners of smaller companies as intruders in their businesses. Both sides of this issue need to be considered whenever you work with a bank or banker.

Finding the right people within a bank may be as simple as walking in and asking. Tell them what you do (assuming that it may be even tangentially related to customer difficulties that they might experience in their small company lending program). Stress your smaller company focus. Find out what they do—their policies and general difficulties. Talk about ways your services might help them to address their customers' (and, hence, their) problems. Leave relevant material, if you have any. Put them on your list for copies of your appropriate speeches or articles. Once you have broken the ice, maintain the relationship.

Interprofessional courtesies often play a significant role in developing these referral relationships. A lawyer I know, for example, recently talked to me about potential financial arrangements that could be made among warring family members within a particular growing retail company. My advice was given gladly, essentially in return for pieces of advice or information that I had received from him earlier. His client could never have been mine in this instance. The issues were short term and the timing made it impossible. Similarly, the clients on whose behalf I had spoken to him were unlikely direct clients for him. But the information and trust basis between the two of us has grown. When a client does need legal advice in an area of his interest, he is naturally the person I think of first. And he refers to me when appropriate.

Such relationships take time and attention, but they are worth it. They not only serve as sources of referral business but they also provide a forum for bouncing ideas around among a number of talented and compatible professionals. This offers not only someone to talk with but also an entirely different set of perspectives on your problem or issue. It is also just plain fun.

OTHER SALES METHODS AND TECHNIQUES

In the consulting books, and in most marketing books, you will also find lists of the X ways to build sales for your company. They are getting short shrift here, simply because, particularly with smaller companies, they don't work very well. The most common suggestions are discussed briefly here.

Cold Calling

The general idea is that you are supposed to knock on doors, talk with the person in charge, and begin a beautiful (and profitable) consulting relationship. These books tell you that the keys to this process are "prospecting" and "qualifying your prospects." You are supposed to determine the characteristics of your potential clientele, select potential companies based on these characteristics, and target them for calls. Of course, it is noted that you will have to knock on X doors and get "no"s for each door behind which you get a "yes." In fact, to thicken your skin and keep your spirits up, you are told to view every "no" as one step closer to the eventual (and inevitable) "yes." I have some doubt that this approach works in any sized company for those of us who sell real intangibles. My experience has shown that even with a more productlike consulting service, it does not work well in smaller companies.

There are any number of difficulties with this approach, many of which grow directly out of the underlying characteristics of most smaller companies.

1. Owners of smaller companies prefer working with those they know and trust.
2. The intangible types of consulting require that an owner or manager tell you her troubles. Is this likely to occur if you simply call on the phone or walk into the office?
3. Without a referral structure for that particular potential client, a cold caller would be at a disadvantage.
4. Cold calling assumes that there is an unlimited supply of potential clients. It also assumes either that the fact that you are pounding the pavement will not get around or that it doesn't matter whether that word gets around. Among smaller companies in a limited geographic or industry area, these assumptions may not be valid. Consider what cold calling may do to your reputation and your image.

As noted, this perspective is tied up with the particular type of consulting you wish to do. If you are selling a service that is more like a product—a computer-based software contract, for example—your odds on this approach would be better. Purchasing from you does not require a great deal of personal involvement or exposure. If, however, you are offering services that will require direct involvement in the owner's company—developing control systems, looking at finances, or reorganizing company functions, for example—there is no substitute for the longer-term development approach described earlier.

Direct Mail

Many books counsel the use of direct mail, alone or in conjunction with a calling program, as a means of selling consulting services. While mailing the potential client something either before or after a telephone call does serve to reinforce whatever you said (or will discuss), the same caveats apply as in a calling program alone.

A direct mail piece as a stand-alone item raises even more difficulties. First, how many of your targets are likely to read the material? Second, how can you convey on paper the sense of trustworthiness and solidity that you can convey in person? More to the point, such campaigns, if done well, are relatively expensive and produce generally low response rates.

Just consider the numbers for a moment. A broad direct mail campaign to sell a product is considered to be a howling success at a response rate of 4–5 percent. Assuming that you have targeted extremely well and get an initial response rate of 5 percent, a gross estimate of your cost is as follows:

Mailing list	$ 400
1,000 mailing pieces printed @ $2	2,000
Postage (bulk rate and postal return)	
@ $0.20	200
Total	2,600

This campaign resulted in fifty initial responses. If your hit rate on initial interviews is one in ten, you will also spend a minimum of 100 hours (excluding travel and preparation time) to make five sales (all of which are likely to appear at about the same time, creating short-term overload for you). This also does not count the time it takes for you to prepare the mailing and shepherd it through whatever subcontractors you use.

Again, if you sell appropriate product kinds of consulting, you might like these numbers. If so, you will need to be sure that your mailing piece is professionally done and that it reflects an appropriate image. Your mailing list supplier will have to be researched and carefully chosen. Mailing lists are notorious for duplicate names, obsolete information, and assorted other difficulties. You will also have to specify *very* carefully the kinds of companies to be included in the list. I learned this the hard way, having once bought a list of small companies in the Pittsburgh area. It seems that the list company read this as "small offices in the Pittsburgh area." On my list were IBM, Air Products, and a host of other giants that had *offices* with fewer than 100 employees in the area. The list was virtually useless to me.

It has also been found that offering a small giveaway increases initial response. You might use one of your relevant reprints or a transcript of one of your speeches. Keep in mind, however, that increasing your initial response does not necessarily increase the total number of projects that flow from such an effort. Most people will cheerfully take almost anything for nothing.

Surveys and Newsletters

For many consultants, these items become businesses in themselves. The general idea is to find topics in your area of expertise that will be of interest to your potential clients, write them up, and send off the results gratis to a qualified prospect list. You include your company's name and how the reader can reach you. They are also often touted as a reminder of your prior services to the company.

The problems and opportunities here are very much like those in the direct mail area. The process is time consuming and costly. Unless the kind of consulting you do is replicable from company to company, these tools are rather unlikely to produce results. The client probably believes that her particular problems are unique. If what you really sell is the problem-solving, company-specific kind of consulting, you may just be wasting time, energy, and money.

Standard Advertising

Some books claim that this can be a useful tool. I have never met a small company client, however, who even reads consultant ads when seeking problem-solving assistance. Here too, however, if your consulting is productlike, there may be some value in this approach. The only advertising I have ever done is support advertising: Buy space in this special edition of X to show your support of the sponsoring group. I have never had a single business-producing response.

The *Yellow Pages*, however, appears to be a unique advertising proposition. Quite a number of owners of smaller companies claim to check there when seeking professional services. While it seems anomalous given the rest of the profile, it exists and professionals should take note and make appropriate arrangements.

Brochures

These can be viewed as sales tools or sales aids. Most books suggest that they are a necessity for building a consulting business. I have never used one. In a very real sense, this is a strategic decision on my part.

Brochures are handy items to leave on tables at meetings or to reinforce your company name at your speaking engagements. Potential clients commonly ask to see company material. At this point, the potential client is often stalling for time or putting you off, however.

To be effective, a brochure must be professional (read *expensive*) and fairly targeted. The practical issue with which you need to deal is whether your service is specific enough to be conveyed effectively in fixed type. Further, you need to decide whether such a statement—with or without pretty pictures—will assist your potential clients in reaching a decision to use your services. I have found that relevant reprints convey the message as well but at lower cost and with the clear imprimatur of an outside professional source: the journal that printed my article or the group that sponsored my presentation. If having a brochure makes *you* feel more legitimate and professional, however, use one. It will be worth the time, effort, and money.

ADVANTAGES OF RELATIONSHIP BUILDING

As you can see, there are numerous approaches to selling consulting services to smaller companies. The method that offers the best possibility for developing long-term consulting relationships with owners of such companies, however, is the one that focuses on relationships as long-term, stable facts in your business life. While it takes longer to grow such relationships with owners, managers, and other professionals, the rewards are large, lasting, and satisfying.

First, if you feel essentially uncomfortable in direct selling situations, the very low-key approach embodied in relationship building will better suit your style and taste. You do not really *sell*; rather, the project or program *evolves* naturally—based on what you and the client agree is really needed.

Second, this method permits you the greatest possible flexibility in responding to the needs of your potential clients. If you make an offer, by advertising, mail, or cold call, it has to be fairly specific. By so doing, you automatically exclude the other kinds of services you might have been able to perform for that client, had you started from what the client needed rather than from what you wanted to sell. You cannot advertise that you will meet any need (particularly if you practice alone or with a small group). Neither can you walk into an office cold and expect to hear about what is really troubling an owner. For this kind of consulting, there really is no substitute for relationship building.

Finally, a client acquired through long-term relationship building is likely to work with you for a long time. Whenever a problem arises that is even tangentially related to your field(s) of expertise (and some that are not), you will hear about it first. Your firm will have the relevant follow-on business, and/or your referrals will be given preferred treatment. Given these advantages, you might want to think of the relationship-based approach to developing sales as an investment of time, energy, and yourself in your business.

4

THE CONSULTING
RELATIONSHIP:
MECHANICS

Assuming that you have been engaged in relationship building, you will immediately be aware of the point at which one of your owners becomes an active prospect for a consulting project. This chapter addresses the issues that may arise between consultant and an owner of a smaller company from that moment to the time at which the consulting work actually begins. It also describes the normal course of the relationship through this period.

This period, the time between acquaintanceship or collegiality and the conclusion of an agreement for you to perform a specific consulting task, is often tricky. It is your job, as the professional in the pair, to make the transition as easy as possible. This requires you to be alert to often subtle signals sent by the owner and to respond to them appropriately. It is also your job to separate clearly your two roles, colleague and expert, so that your client can be comfortable in both relationships with you.

It is impossible to discuss all the possible permutations of these situations. What this chapter tries to do is to help you become aware of the issues and undercurrents that frequently occur during this period in a nascent consulting relationship. Using this information, and the sample approaches outlined, you will be better able to recognize critical points in the process and to tailor your responses to your specific situation. It also offers some fairly detailed discussion of issues common to virtually all new consulting relationships—setting prices, for example—and offers some assistance in making your decisions about handling them.

HOW DO YOU KNOW WHEN THE TIME IS RIGHT?

When an owner/manager begins to consider you for a change in relationship from friendly outsider to consultant, a shift will take place in the way she deals with you. She may begin to ask fairly specific questions about former clients or the content of prior projects you have performed in specific fields. She will already have indicated general interest in that particular area. She may ask you to come out and have a look at the plant or store or office. She may suggest meeting you for lunch or breakfast without an agenda relating to the organization or issue you already have in common. These are fairly clear signals that something is about to change.

In other situations, the change may be very small. She might, for example, ask business questions of you in a slightly different tone than the one she used to use or appear to evaluate your responses differently. Alternatively, the questions might begin to relate to a specific issue in her business rather than to general business or company topics. In short, you need to be alert to any changes in nuance. In general, it is better to operate as if the point of change has been reached and probe for confirmation than to miss or ignore a signal that the client probably believes is blatant.

Reaching the transition point in an existing relationship should never come as a complete surprise to you. You know your potential client. He has been talking with you on and off over the past X weeks, months, or years. You probably know what business he is in and something about his business as well. He will have evidenced interest in specific areas of business or business issues during that period. Questions at meetings will show clear directions and interests. This person is not a mystery to you.

All the small signals and bits of information will have been heard by you (assuming you were really listening). They will have been stored away in the filing section of your mind (or on cards or disks, if you're so inclined). Each new bit of information will be added to your overall image until you have in your mind a fairly coherent pattern for this person. Thus, when you begin to sense that your potential client is sending signals, you will already have a fair sense of what the questions are likely to be about, how you might be able to provide assistance, and what might be needed.

While this process of listening, cataloging, and reconfiguring sounds time consuming and largely fruitless, it becomes a habit of mind that you will find natural after a remarkably short time. Think of all the patterns you discern that never turn into business as practice. The process is important, however, to keep you ready to talk business with a potential client when required. You need to update these images and patterns of potential clients continually so you will always be reasonably prepared to make the shift to consultant. As is said, "The best answer to an unexpected question is the one you thought of last night."

Note: This approach also works, though of course not as well, when you have no previous relationship with a potential client. If someone you do not know approaches you—she's heard you speak, read your work, knows a previous client—your pattern-building period is simply highly condensed. You must take your readings quickly. You probably know more than you think about this new person. You know, for example, the person who suggested she call. Or you know what she reads. Or you know at least one organization to which she belongs. Getting into the habit of fitting pieces together as recommended will be especially helpful in these situations.

When you believe that a potential client is beginning to approach you as a possible consultant for his business, your response may both encourage him to do so and set the tone for your new relationship. Therefore, your response counts. In response to the signals, you are supposed to become slightly (emphasize *slightly*) more professional and expertlike by contrast to the friendly, collegial approach you have adopted to that point. This will let your potential client know that you have noted the shift and will also give you an opportunity to probe *gently* for what is really going on without endangering either the potential project (if any) or the existing relationship. If you make your response totally open-ended ("It sounds as if you have something specific on your mind"), the potential client retains his options and you retain yours.

There are a number of things you should definitely *not* do at this turning point in the relationship. First, no matter *how* long you have been hoping and dreaming about getting into this particular company, do not pant or look otherwise overanxious. As they say in the antiperspirant commercials, "Never let them see you sweat."

Moreover, do not start coming up with glib answers to your potential client's more specific questions. This reaction is fairly common since, suddenly, you are trying to impress a potential client rather than to talk with an acquaintance. There are two major reasons for squelching this response. First and most obvious, if the problem can be solved over coffee in ten minutes, either you have blown the real consulting project or there really is no project. Second, and more important from a longer-term perspective, your potential client is truly troubled and/or baffled by the problem he is raising tentatively with you. If you rattle off thirty solutions in ten seconds or less, he is likely to feel like an idiot. Nobody is likely to work willingly with someone who makes him feel stupid. And your client is the buyer.

Finally, don't talk, listen. This is critical, in any case, to being a good consultant, but it is particularly important now. Your potential client is trying out his problem statement and checking your reaction(s). He is also trying on the notion of really working with you. Your job at this point is to help him clarify the problem and, if necessary, to bring what you believe might be the main problem(s) more centrally into focus for him.

Do not worry about whether he understands that you are the world's foremost expert on X. If he has checked you out, he probably already knows. If he has not checked you out, he probably doesn't particularly care. In short, do not beat him over the head with your expertise. If it is really there, it will show in the way you address the problem he is raising with you. If he is smart, he is probably assessing your responses in terms of how you bring your experience to bear on the problem he has raised and how well and rapidly you make relevant connections among pieces of the problem as he outlines it. You excel, at this point, by judicious, probing questions, not by making pronouncements. Assume your potential client is smart.

THE NEXT STEPS: INITIAL INTERVIEWS

Once you determine that you are probably discussing a real potential project with a real potential client, you need to do two things. First, you need to move the discussion to a place in which your potential

client feels comfortable. This is likely to be her office. Second, you
need to define the project.

A Place to Talk

Believe it or not, a key decision in the process may be where you
hold your initial meetings. First, there is the issue of client comfort
(mental, not physical). There is also the issue of access to information—and, sometimes, information itself—involved in the decision.
There are three basic options: your office, her office, or some neutral
ground.

Many consultants feel most comfortable at initial interviews in
their own offices. Assuming they have read all the books about pro-
jecting an appropriate image, their offices will properly impress the
potential client with their successes and expertise. This choice is
usually the wrong one for those of us who work with owners of smaller
companies. Most likely, your office (if you have a proper one) has
been designed to impress. It is probably grander than that of your
potential client. The consultant is showing off in a general way, and
most owners of smaller companies are ever alert to such nuances. The
potential client may be intimidated. At best, he is on unfamiliar
territory, is somewhat uncertain and, therefore, less likely to talk
freely.

A second consideration for consultants who work with owners of
smaller companies is the constant attention to what things—particularly consulting services, cost. If you have clearly spent massive
amounts to furnish an office, your potential client may question your
priorities and wonder whether there is any way to afford your services. You do not want him thinking in those ways at that point. Your
goal should be client comfort and ease. If you really feel the need to
show your level of success, do so in smaller ways—your briefcase,
your watch, the cut of your suit, etc. Make it an aura instead of a
sledge hammer.

The second choice is often some neutral ground. Depending on
the nature of the problem your potential client appears to want to
discuss, an out-of-the-office site might be appropriate. Once you
decide that might be the case, the next question is which of you
chooses the place. It is generally better, again for reasons of promot-
ing client comfort, to let your potential client choose. If you take over

the decision immediately, you have taken control of the process from the potential client. That is likely to be frightening.

If your potential client asks you to name the place, do so with care. If you suggest "my club," questions of fees and tastes arise again. If "your club" happens to be associated with money, privilege, and/or a top-flight school, the intimidation factor goes to work again. Try to match your choice to where you think your potential client is. You have probably met before at various functions, so you have some notion of the kinds of places he is used to. Beyond those considerations, the only requirements of the place include a reasonable level of quiet and a reasonable amount of space between tables. It also helps if you know that the staff will not try to hustle you out as soon as your coffee appears. Again, the objective is to maximize client comfort.

The issue of who pays comes up at this point. The issue of the check is one reason why "my club" or "his club" is a preferred location for such meetings. The signature system of most clubs obviates the entire issue. The member of the club pays—at month end, when the bill arrives.

The potential client has some reason for believing that he should handle the bill. He has not yet decided to bring you in and, therefore, wishes to maintain control, owe you absolutely nothing, and demonstrate both. Since he has not made the decision, he may still feel that he is in the picking-your-brain stage and should buy as a means of recompense for services received. All this is, of course, informal and generally unspoken. (If your potential client is female, she may also need to let you know that she does not expect special treatment because of that fact. Picking up the check is an easy, clear way for her to make that statement.)

On the other hand, you are stalking a potential client. The seeker of business is the traditional bill payer. That means you. Nevertheless the issue of client comfort should dictate what you choose to do. It is generally wise to make the first move toward the check yourself, indicating your willingness to buy. If you detect discomfort in your potential client or the beginning of a minor argument, let the client do it.

The final location option—and my favorite—is at the office of your potential client. It gets my vote for three main reasons. First, he is likely to feel most comfortable on his own turf. Second, you can see him in his normal surroundings. If you pay attention, you can glean a lot of possibly useful and relevant information from the layout and furnishings of the place and from how he interacts with other company personnel (and how they react to him). Third, should any data, documents, or input from other personnel be needed in your initial clarification discussion, they will be handy. You will also be able, should you conclude an agreement, to leave with the material you need to begin your work. The less time between agreement and results, the better.

How to Discuss the Project

Actually, your main job in the initial discussions with a potential client is not talking, but listening. Active listening requires that you ask relevant, helpful questions that assist in shaping a useful working definition of the problem or issue with which the client wants you to deal. This problem definition phase is necessary to the performance and conclusion of a successful consulting project. Both of you must be extremely clear about what is to be done and what will result from your proposed activity. In the absence of such definition, the process or the result is likely to be unsatisfactory. If your work does not satisfy the client, not only do you lose the potential for follow-on and/or referral business but you also may not get paid.

First, as you listen, take mental notes—physical ones, if you prefer *and* if your prospective client does not mind. Ask before you pull out pad and pen. You are seeking two kinds of information. You need to know what the owner believes is the problem. You also need to know as much about the owner and the business as possible. Thus, the questions you ask should be very broad and open-ended.

Second, as you listen, consider other work you have done that may be relevant to the kinds of difficulties the client is describing to you. Your thoughts should *not* be oriented toward impressing the client with your experience directly; rather, they should concentrate on connections that you found that were not immediately obvious or on auxiliary issues that arose in the course of your work. The difficult part of this is not to let your thought patterns drown out what the client is telling you. In short, you need to learn to "multi-program."

This ability is rather like the ability to fit pieces of people-puzzles together on the fly, as discussed earlier. It improves with practice. Besides, if you have taken the comments about preparation to heart, you will have a fair notion about the topics of discussion before you actually sit down with the client. Thus, you will have worked out most of the possible project interrelations in advance. Until you reach the point where you can sort through your data banks *and* listen with a reasonable level of facility, however, listening to the client should take absolute precedence.

Finally, *never* say anything without thinking about it first. The thought process can be brief. A few seconds is generally sufficient to frame what you want to say or ask in words you choose to use. But the pause should occur. It will ensure that you say only what you mean to say. The person with whom you are talking will not notice your thinking time as a real pause. In fact, you will appear careful and deliberate rather than slow.

If you think about the purposes of this initial meeting (and subsequent meetings) with a client, the reasons for this level of care will be apparent. First, you do not want to "step on the client's lines." Jumping in with comment—however brilliant—will make your potential client nervous. He may have been about to tell you something that would have made *him* look brilliant (and you spoiled his fun). Or he might have been about to tell you something that makes hash of your wonderful theory (in which case you look pretty stupid). Even if neither would have occurred, you have clearly moved to take control at a point when he has not yet decided to relinquish it to you. His perfectly reasonable next thought is likely to be whether he wants anybody as precipitous as you wandering around loose in his company. A brief pause before you speak lets you be certain that the client is finished saying whatever he was going to say.

Perhaps more to the point, you are there to establish a business relationship with this potential client. The client has invited you in to discuss what might become the terms of your deal. Anything you say in those meetings is likely to be thought of by the client as part of your agreement with her—and appropriately so, since you *did* say it. Until you have explored sufficiently, then, you want to make no promises, either implied or explicit. Careful framing of your questions, comments, and statements can be critical in making no implied guarantees or promises.

Asking the Right Questions

As noted before, asking the right questions is a central skill in your bag of techniques as a consultant. At the transition point between colleague and professional, your skills in this area might really make the difference between landing and losing the project.

Your questions should be aimed at clarification of what the problem might be or what the specific job is that the owner wants done. Working with the owner, you want to target potential problem areas and/or limit, in some manner, the areas you will need to deal with. Particularly if you sense that the problem the owner is describing may not be the real problem, your questions need to be gently probing, even statementlike: "I have found that in X-industry companies, overinvestment in capacity is common." This is nonjudgmental (and stresses your relevant experience). You hope that the owner will begin to discuss how relevant that observation is to his company. If possible, you want the owner to believe that he, himself, has discovered that a broader field of inquiry would be appropriate for addressing the difficulties in his operation.

If the very gentle, leading approach does not work, test a straightforward question: "Have you considered the possibility that . . . ?" If your prospective client really bristles at the very suggestion, you may have a problem in performing the project properly. He may well have some personal investment in the status quo in an area that you suspect will require major changes. This should raise red flags for you if your strategy has been to get him to address the right basic issues. At this point, if you choose, you might shift strategies to limiting your proposed project to very specific goals, results, and/or investigations that can be accomplished without treading on that especially sensitive area.

Despite appearances to the contrary, the point of this questioning/defining exercise is not to give the client free information or to impress the client with your abilities (though it does do some of both). Its purpose is self-protection in its most basic form. In a real sense, you depend on the client's satisfaction for payment (unless you plan to spend your life in various courts of law). Unless each of you has a pretty good idea about what you are getting into, that satisfaction is far from assured—no matter how technically fantastic your performance may be. Consider a hypothetical case.

Suppose, for example, that your prospective client believes that her problem relates to poor company sales. The more you listen, the more you believe that the real issues may lie in the way the company invests in assets. Since it has too many assets, a perfectly reasonable sales level would be inadequate to support them. You and the owner make a deal. She thinks you are addressing a sales problem. You are addressing an asset problem (assuming you have proven your initial suspicions correct). When you present your results/report, is she going to be pleased? Did you solve her problem?

If the problem was defined (by default, in this case) as a sales problem, the owner will not be satisfied. You have not solved the problem—that is, you have not figured out how to produce more sales. You have, of course, come up with a brilliant approach to making the current level of sales adequate by reducing asset investment, but that was not the problem the owner thought you were dealing with.

This may all sound a bit apocryphal to you. After all, one would expect the owner of a company, being closest to it, to understand it best and target its problems well. In reality, however, this appears not to be the case for most owners of smaller companies. A colleague and I recently studied all the clients of one area's Small Business Administration-supported assistance program. When we compared the problems as initially described by owners with those described by the professional consultants who worked with them, we found that they did not match in more than 70 percent of the cases. This finding confirmed our experiences in working with owners of smaller companies. Discussions with still other colleagues provided additional anecdotal evidence for the notion that owners often target the wrong problem.

In real life, the best way to head off an end result that is at cross-purposes with the owner is to address *as a possibility* the issue *you* think might be the problem early in the consulting relationship. You are likely to save yourself (and the owner) a great deal of hassle and grief by doing one of two things. In the hypothetical case described earlier, you might have tried, through raising relevant questions, to get the owner to see the possible relationship between her beautiful new headquarters building and the inadequacy of sales. Alternatively, you could have limited your work to developing approaches to increasing sales (and have set expected results in concrete terms not related to "adequacy"). However, unless you explicitly defined what you were to do for this company at the outset, the likelihood of not meeting the owner's expectation was high.

Such situations leave you, as the professional, with a choice. Essentially, you can either assist the owner to deal with the right problem or limit your responsibility for the real problem by setting very tightly defined results for the project you will perform. In either case, a clear project definition will help.

In choosing which approach to take, your consulting strategy and philosophy should help you make the choice. I prefer the admittedly riskier course of trying to convince the owner that the problem may be broader than or different from the one he has focused on. I have found that even meeting the stated objectives—if they are the wrong objectives—will not really satisfy the client or make the company inherently stronger. Since those are my personal priorities, I rarely take on a project in which I cannot help the client address what I believe to be the real issues. I find it depressing to expend energy—even for money—to address an issue that will make no headway toward solving a company's real problems.

Project Definition

The substance of your project definition will vary of course, depending on your particular field(s) of expertise. There are, however, a number of general items that should be part of any project description. After a general comment on project definitions, each is discussed briefly in this section.

A project definition should reflect the essence of what you and your client agree to do for each other in the course of your work with her company. If well done, it will serve as both protection for you and an outline for your client. I am extremely wary of a client (or another consultant, for that matter) who is unwilling to define projects and commit to the definitions. On the part of a consultant, it may well indicate significant uncertainty about the probability of producing the desired results. On the part of a client, it may well signal that the content of the project is not really decided at all. For a consultant who tries to perform on such a project, the results can be disastrous. The task is likely to change from day to day or from moment to moment. Whatever is produced is likely to be the wrong something. A good project definition can preclude a great deal of trouble by the simple expedient of providing boundaries—in both time and subject matter—for a project.

This is not to say that, as you and your client progress into the project, the definition cannot be changed. If you have written it down and agreed to it, however, changing it should be done by further discussions and an amended agreement. While this sounds legalistic, it is merely prudent. If one of you makes a change to which the other really does not agree, you could wind up back where you started, with you and your client expecting different results from the project. Neither of you would be satisfied in the long run.

To best serve its purposes, a good project definition should have five clear parts. First, it should describe the broad objective of the assistance you will provide for the client. Second, it should describe in some detail the process you intend to follow to assist the client in meeting the objective. Third, it should detail any limitations to which both parties have agreed. Fourth, it should state what the client is responsible for providing to your joint effort. Fifth, it should describe the form of the results that you will present to the client during and at the end of the process. Essentially, it should reflect the totality of your agreement.

Objective statement.   The broad objective statement is often useful in reminding both parties of what you intended to do when you began the project. While that sounds as if it should be unnecessary, if a project is large and/or complex, periodic reminders can really help to keep everyone focused and on track. If the overall purpose of the project will be embraced by company employees, an objective statement may even be helpful in enlisting cooperation or enthusiasm from the troops. If nothing else, it may help defuse the normal concerns and resentments of having an outsider poking around in their departments.

Process description.   The process description serves a number of purposes. It helps you to work out the shape of the project in advance of actually doing it. This will help in your cost-estimating process and, therefore, should be done even if you and the client do not write it into your agreement. If you do write it down (and I argue that you should), a process description will alert people in relevant departments or areas of the company to when you are likely to appear and what you are likely to want when you get there. It will minimize their uncertainty and give them time to prepare and, if you are lucky, to come up with helpful suggestions. (Listen. It can't hurt.)

The process description is often an area of some concern to consultants. It could, theoretically, provide the reader with a blueprint for performing the project herself or with internal personnel. It need not be that detailed, however. What you want is for this section to reflect the broad sweep of your work rather than the minutiae. "Analyze the content of X tasks in the Y process" is specific but hardly adequate to permit the client to complete the task, even assuming adequate numbers of personnel. The goal, again, is to strike a balance between specificity and massive detail.

Once in a while, another consultant will use your process description to perform the work for less money. When that occurs, just write it off—and keep an eye on that other consultant. Your continued equanimity will embarrass your client for a good long time, but only if you maintain your cordial attitude.

Limitations. The limitations, or caveats, section is a clear form of protection for you. In it should go any items or issues that you and the client have agreed are out of bounds for this particular project. It should also include any other limitations on the scope of the project and any issues that you would normally expect to have addressed that for reasons of client money or preference you will not address.

A clear statement of limitations, agreed to by your client, may stave off major distress at the results of a project. I recall a project in which a client split a project in what I considered an unrealistic manner. I stated that his choice about how to spend his consulting dollars was a poor one and that the lines should have been drawn differently. He insisted and it was, after all, his money. When it turned out, as I had suspected, that the part he wanted done was relatively useless without the part he had excluded, what saved me was the clear, signed statement to the effect that that crucial part had been excluded from the beginning. This was certainly not a good solution, but it did beat having him accuse me of not doing the job I had agreed to perform.

Requirements of the client. Can you really do this project entirely on your own (with your own staff)? Or will you need some things from the client company? The second situation is far more likely and should be clear in your project definition. Both what you will need from the client organization and when you will need it should be written down in whatever level of detail is appropriate. Most likely, your needs will relate to staff time and company data. It should be clear that the project will not be completed properly (or on time) without access to the agreed-upon resources from the client. (Funding, which is also part of the client commitment, is really a separate subject. It is treated as such in this chapter under "Billing and Collections.")

Output.   Finally, your project definition should describe the form(s) and timing of the results you both expect from your project. These are the output, or the deliverables, or whatever they are called in your field. While you will not be able to define their specific contents until you do the project, the descriptions should include the general subject area(s) and, if relevant, the structure or format of your reporting mechanism—a presentation, a draft, a final report, etc.

The times to which you agree are firm deadlines. As noted earlier, meeting these deadlines is critical to your longer-term success with this client (and his referral group). It is not (or should not be) acceptable for you to explain on deadline day that Charlie Jones did not get you the material he was responsible for getting you. It was up to you to see that Charlie got the material to you in time. By deadline day, it is *all* your responsibility.

OTHER ISSUES

The Formal Arrangement

The form of this project description is up to you. Some consultants seem to like a formal contract. Some even have developed fill-in-the-blanks forms. If you like that approach, use it, but incorporate your specific project definition by referring to it and attaching it to the contract form. Check with your lawyer.

I have found that, in general, a letter of understanding (LOU) is simpler and as effective in protecting your interests. It may not be quite as solid if you expect to have to haul your client into court. The question then becomes, of course, Are you really likely to sue the guy if the agreement falls apart? If your answer is "yes," then go with a true contract. If not, why not take the easier way?

An LOU has certain advantages in addition to its simplicity. First, its very informality is less threatening to your client. She may feel that she has to call her lawyer about a true contract. She may simply accept an agreement made through an LOU; after all, you worked it out together. Second, it is likely to be quicker in getting you to work. An LOU need not even demand a client countersignature since it really does reflect mutual agreement. It is a record of an existing understanding. You can send it and start. Finally, but certainly not least, it offers endless flexibility of form. You do not have to fit your agreement into legalistically contractual terms.

This stress on reducing the legalistic nature of the formal arrangement should not be read to indicate that no formal statement is needed. The point is simply that, within reasonable limits, informal formality is as likely to get you where you want to go as a legal contract. And it is likely to get you there faster and with less haggling.

The key to writing a good LOU is to reflect, as well and as clearly as you can, your understanding of what you and the client agreed on. It is *not* the time to add some little items you had forgotten (or wanted to change). You do want the client to react if your understandings of what was agreed on differ. You do not want the client to balk because you added things you did not discuss or agree about beforehand. Adding at that stage not only will create entirely avoidable delays but also will make you appear sneaky to the client. She might reasonably presume that there was some nefarious reason that you did not discuss or raise the items you added unilaterally. In truth, if anyone tried that with me as client, I would throw him out of my office on general principles. End of project. When a client (who has managed to obtain the task of preparing the LOU, or scope of work, or whatever) tries to alter our actual agreements, I am quite likely to refuse the project entirely.

This raises the question of which party should prepare the LOU or the project statement. Even when the project began with a request for proposals (RFP) from the client, I try to take responsibility for writing the project definition/contract scope of work/LOU. While the choice is yours, I have found that the times I have been lax in insisting that we do the draft have been the times in which it took forever to reach a not-quite-satisfactory agreement about project definition.

There are a number of simple reasons for this phenomenon. First, given that clients frequently focus on the wrong problems or issues, preparing the draft or the letter myself ensures the proper emphases. The process also gives me another opportunity to lay the logic of my priorities before the client—a reiteration that cannot hurt. Second, since I am the one (or the leader of the group) who will be performing the project work, I am likely to be better able to describe the process, the timing, the requirements, and the output. Finally, if

I prepare it, I am in control of the time frame for delivery of the LOU. I am not waiting to receive a client piece to which to react. This generally speeds and simplifies the entire process.

Getting Paid

Getting paid is clearly an issue close to the hearts (and stomachs) of both consultants and clients. I have split the discussion of payment into two main parts and one purely mechanical part. The part in this chapter includes some discussion of pricing mechanisms and general billing/collections provisions of your contract or LOU. Since pricing is also a strategic issue for consultants, additional discussion is offered in Chapter 10. Appendix B provides descriptions and worksheets for some standard pricing calculations.

The issue of how and when you get paid for your work is an important part of your written agreement with your client. While it is unlikely that your client will fail to ask you about your charges and cost estimates in the discussion phase, it *has* occurred. If necessary, bring up the topic yourself—after all, it will be your work, your staff and expenses, and your money. In this area, in particular, your draft letter should not come as a shock to your client.

Pricing approaches.   When the topic is raised, you have three basic options about your pricing approach: (1) fixed fee, (2) a per diem arrangement, or (3) some kind of performance-based arrangement. My strong preference is always for a per diem arrangement. I insist on this mechanism unless there is some legal reason (client's) for making some other arrangement.

The reasons for this insistence are clear if you consider the implications of each mechanism for your eventual payment times and levels. A basic underlying issue is which party takes the risks inherent in performing any project. Under a per diem arrangement, your client takes the risk. Under a fixed price arrangement, you bear all the risk. In my view, in most instances, the former arrangement is more appropriate.

While this may appear merely self-serving, consider the situation dispassionately. You have made certain assumptions about conditions at the client company in your pricing estimates. You assumed, for example, an average level of data availability or a normal level of record keeping. When you find that data is virtually unusable or records nonexistent, which party should bear the costs of compensating for the deficiency?

Clients naturally prefer to shift the risk to you through a fixed price arrangement. They fear that you have low-balled your estimates of time and fees. You will, in their nightmares, announce one day that your fees are roughly triple what you estimated, and that you will try to shift the blame to their people or systems besides. Do *not* take this attitude personally. There *are* consultants who do this kind of thing. Under a per diem arrangement, the exposure is real, and trust, in business, goes only so far. A relatively simple way to allay client fears in this area is to offer a hybrid arrangement that limits client exposure somewhat. A per diem agreement with a not-to-exceed limit usually fills the bill. In it, you agree that you will bill on a time-and-expenses basis up to a specified limit. Thereafter, the risk is yours.

I have dealt with this problem by really honing my estimating skills and by performing assessments of relevant client systems/data/ etc., when possible, prior to developing estimates. Whether or not I mention it to my clients, my estimate is, in my view, a not-to-exceed price. Only under extremely adverse conditions that I could not reasonably have foreseen will I exceed my estimates appreciably. Clients do *not* get upset when you bring a project in *under* budget.

This leaves us with a third broad approach to pricing. Performance-based pricing has recently become very popular with writers on consulting. The general idea is that you do your work and then get either a percentage of savings, sales, etc. as your fee or you get an agreed-upon amount when you have performed to specifications. The seduction lies in the notion that the sale is easier since the client pays nothing unless she gets specific, quantified results. The project, in effect, pays you itself.

While seductive, this is a dangerous notion for both consultants and clients to play with. Most old-line consulting firms find it unprofessional and will not do it. Many deem it unethical to profit through their clients—even in this manner. Proponents of this approach consider this attitude a reflection of concern about being judged on the basis of performance.

My difficulties regarding this payment mechanism are more practical than ethical. Consider the problem for a consultant, an outsider in a particular company. Assume, for example, that you base your consulting deal on increasing sales by X percent or Y dollars. How will you know whether you have succeeded? You could let the client tell you. This is unsatisfactory, since there is no established mechanism for her to do so. (Also, you may not trust her to be entirely forthcoming about how much she owes you.) Your alternative is to audit the sales figures of this client. Do you really want to spend your time (and anger your former client) by bringing in your accountants? Those, however, are your alternatives for getting paid.

Suppose you base your payment on opening and penetrating a new market. You are to do the market research, develop the marketing plan, etc. You then get to sit and wait for payment until the client implements your plan. You can limit this wait through a clause setting a time limit on implementation. Such a clause would specify that you will be paid in case the client decides, despite your recommendation, not to go ahead with the program. (You, of course, are left with the issue of not getting paid for your effort should you conclude that the program should not go ahead. Herein lies the basis for a significant conflict. Do you tell the client and skip your fees?)

While you can limit your exposure to client decisions not to proceed, under a performance-based arrangement you are still tied to the client's ability to implement your plans properly and well. As a consultant, you are, by definition, not in control of the operation of the business. When you accept a performance-based pricing mechanism, you are placing your faith (not to mention your dinner and mortgage) in the willingness and ability of others to implement your programs. That is not a position in which I care to be. In fact, it is one of the major reasons I left corporate life. The choice is yours, however, for your business.

Billing and collections.   While most clients agree with the best will in the world to pay you, frequent facts of life in smaller companies are severely restricted cash flows and periodic cash shortages. Since you are neither a vital supplier nor do you deal in hard goods, it is entirely likely that you will be among the first victims of such shortages. That being the case, this section addresses two issues to consider as you conclude a consulting agreement: (1) billing and collections and (2) when to quit.

Your normal billing arrangements should be clearly stated in your written agreement with your client (and mentioned in your initial discussions). A critical notion here is that your time and the time of your staff, once used, cannot be recaptured. It is the original perishable item. As such, payment for it at relatively frequent intervals is highly recommended. Even if your own cash flows do not demand frequent payment, you should seek it from your clients for two reasons. First, it is a method of gauging commitment to the project in which you are engaged. Second, it ensures that you are aware of the likelihood of payment before you have gotten too far into project work.

My standard statement about my billing practices is, "It is our practice to bill clients on a monthly basis for professional time expended and for out-of-pocket expenses incurred in performing project services." There are, unfortunately, no hard and fast rules about how to proceed if your initial bills elicit no check in response. You just have to make a series of judgment calls involving one very tangible issue and a number of intangible ones.

The tangible one has to do with the cash requirements of the project from my company. The amount of actual cash expended on behalf of a client—expenses, subcontractors, etc.—is important because it affects my cash flow and my ability to pay my suppliers and contractors. If the project has cost me money and is likely to continue to require a relatively high level of up-front cash from my company, I am likely to cut my losses earlier. If my expenditures are already largely over, I am likely to slow down the professional time commitment and hope to recoup something.

The best method is never to find yourself in this position regarding up-front expenses. This may be accomplished by asking your clients for some funding at the beginning of your project to cover out-of-pocket expenses, if nothing else. Depending on the client and the project, this may be perfectly acceptable. Moreover, the response may give you a real clue about the likelihood of this client's paying you in the end.

The intangible issues tend to be more difficult. I tend to be more flexible, for example, with long-time clients and with clients who call to explain delays in payment. I am also more tolerant of delays in payment when the client has already paid for part of the project. In short, I am relatively tolerant if there appears to be a good-faith intention to pay and the probability of payment in the relatively near future.

Despite my judgments of good faith, I will never deliver final product before most of the payment is in hand. Moreover, I try to delay delivery of *any* product or results until some payment has been received. This is merely prudent. While I consider my judgment of people to be reasonably good, I have been (and I expect I will be in the future) wrong sometimes. Limiting losses by withholding project results to induce payment is one way of insuring against the consequences of such errors.

The process described in this chapter is essentially a continuation of the approach described in Chapter 3. It proposes a fairly relaxed approach to the transition from colleague or acquaintance to consultant. The major issues confronting both parties in making the transition successfully include becoming comfortable with the new relationship, defining the work that needs to be done, and structuring an arrangement that shares risk and responsibility (including payment for services rendered) appropriately. The next chapter takes a brief look at how to operate in situations that are not so relaxed and natural.

5

THE CONSULTING PROCESS: WHAT'S GOING ON BETWEEN YOU AND YOUR CLIENT?

Once you have a signed agreement to perform a consulting project, you're in, right? Once you actually begin, doing work within the company becomes easier since the company is smaller, right? Once the owner/manager accepts you, you're in great shape, right?

Well, not necessarily. Signing a piece of paper often appears to mean less in a smaller company than in a larger one. This has nothing to do with regard (or the lack thereof) for legal formalities. It only rarely has anything to do with you, personally. When difficulties occur in beginning consulting situations, the root cause is generally in the structure and/or the dynamics of the smaller company. This is also one of the major reasons that I noted in the last chapter that the less time there is between agreement and beginning, the better it is for you.

This is not to say that you can do nothing to make the situation in general, and your project in particular, easier in most cases. Nor is it to say that you may not choose to adjust your personal style to achieve a better working fit in smaller companies. Rather, the thrust of this chapter is to help you to make the most of your consulting opportunities in smaller companies. It concentrates on helping you become aware of the underlying issues with which you are dealing so you can take appropriate steps.

The chapter offers assistance by providing analysis of what often happens inside smaller companies and information about how those situations affect a working consultant. It discusses various approaches to addressing some of the more common situations consultants face in their working relationships in smaller companies. Awareness of issues and good starting places for dealing with them are, I believe, critical factors in converting potentially hazardous—or at least significantly annoying and distracting—situations.

INFORMATION REQUIREMENTS

Working with smaller companies usually means that there will be different information requirements than there are in larger companies. As the consultant, you will need information to perform your tasks. It is often the case in smaller companies that the data you need will be difficult to come by or to organize in a relevant manner. On the other side of the consulting transaction, the owner/manager is likely to want (need) more, different, and more frequent information feedback than a large-company manager. In fact, maintaining a sizable and relevant information flow is one way of buying relative freedom from interruption when performing project work in smaller companies.

Consultant

People in smaller companies tend to write less down. This tendency poses a problem for consultants, who generally require information to proceed with their project tasks. The paucity of written records may stem from a number of factors, depending on the particular company.

1. The company may be very new and have virtually no recorded history.
2. If it is very simply organized, the normal records requirements made of most companies by various government agencies (e.g., IRS, employment, etc.) may not apply.
3. The company may have largely long-time staff, all of whom just carry information around in their heads. ("Talk to Jack. He knows everything about. . . .")

4. Everybody may know everybody else very well. When information exchange occurs on a highly informal basis (however complete), the information is rarely in written form.

5. The owner may be concerned about information leaks to competitors or to the business community at large.

Your first job as you begin a consulting project, of course, is to find the requisite data and to pry it loose for your use. In this process, it is often vital to understand why the information you need is not written down or organized appropriately. Unless you know why, you are likely to have no good lever for getting it out.

Consider the case of the consultant who wanted to look at supplier accounts to address an issue of poor profitability. She found supplier volumes, shipments, and payments in an appropriate tabular format. When she sought backup purchase orders, invoices, correspondence, etc., however, there was little to be found. Requests for the backup material met with clear unwillingness to discuss the lack.

Had she discovered massive fraud? Had she trod on sensitive competitive material? Had she exposed major flaws in company information management? As it turned out, she had merely uncovered a major case of company embarrassment. A new purchasing person had recently come on board to professionalize a largely ad hoc buying operation. The people who had been doing the purchasing found that they had been failing to make good use of the system and were generally unhappy with their performance. They closed ranks against the outsiders.

As is often the case, closing ranks here meant manipulating the data. Everything required for tax and accounting reporting was, of course, untouched. That information would not, in any case, have revealed the failures the employees were trying to cover. The backup, however, had gotten "lost", or misfiled, or "Bruce must have taken it when he left. Is it important?"

While the story itself is extreme, consider its implications for the consultant in getting to the information she needed. Had she concluded, for example, that fraud was occurring, she might well have gone to the owner (assuming she believed that he was not in on the game). This might have resulted in the permanent "loss" of the records—not to mention a major row in the company. The ultimate result would have been project failure and, possibly, the beginning of a consultant's reputation for being disruptive.

Had she concluded that records had been buried in the name of corporate secrecy, a trip to the owner would have been unlikely to help. Most such notions of secrecy come directly from owners. Her approach then might have been to stress the trust already placed in her, to promise to maintain secrecy (and not to copy records and take them away), and to explain her purposes. It might have worked, but circumventing the owner (client) carries clear pitfalls of its own.

This consultant, however, put together the recent arrival of the new purchasing person with the general attitudes and training levels of the old-timers and reached the right conclusion. Her approach (which produced the required records) was to stress her task—to increase the profitability of the company's sales—and to downplay her need to point fingers at past errors. She added liberal helpings of sympathy for past lack of knowledge and cheers for the rapid progress of their learning. She got her information with relatively little fuss.

To accomplish this feat, she needed to be aware of the recent acquisition of the professional purchasing person. She also had to be aware of the backgrounds of the employees in areas of the company relevant to her work. In short, she had to have been listening carefully to the owner as he talked about the company in general, as well as noting the details that were directly relevant to her defined project. She had to have been listening between the lines. *And* she had to have been shaping her working model of company operations in her mind as she went along, putting it all together.

This vignette demonstrates the critical notion in information gathering for consultants. Take at least marginal note of *everything*. You never know when it will be very handy for you to know something. And it can't hurt.

It is also good practice to run open projects, sharing relevant information among relevant employees as you develop/discover it. Part of the implied deal between the consultant discussed previously and the old-timers, in fact, was that whatever she came up with that might help them improve their performance would be fed back to them quickly.

My general assumption (borne out in this vignette and in long practice) is that employees usually want to do a good job—particularly if it is as easy as doing a poor one. Thus, any information that you can provide to help them do so will benefit all parties. The employee(s) will learn. The company will do better. You will be viewed as one who helps and, thus, will have better access to more information, opinion, and support.

Determining whether a truly open project is feasible given the particular company and project in which you are involved may be the difficult part of this recommendation. The assumption of a general desire to do well might not be shared by your owner/client. Alternatively, the information you are using might be (or be felt by him to be) clearly sensitive or confidential.

Two methods are suggested for deciding how to approach information dissemination issues. First, your common sense must guide you. What you have already heard from the owner and what you already know about him should also be assessed in this process. Second, talk directly with your client about how he feels about information sharing. As is discussed at greater length later, most owners of smaller companies tend to be either extremely open, running their companies on informal, collegial bases, or extremely wary of permitting *anyone* to know anything about company issues.

Your initial discussions with your client will alert you to her basic tendency. As you move to close the sale and begin the project, it is wise to ask, specifically, who is permitted to know what. If, at the outset or at any time during your work, you have significant disagreements with policy, try explaining your position. You will, of course, need compelling logical and/or practical arguments for it, since you are suggesting a change in one of the more basic pieces of the client's management style.

If you fail to convince her of the essential rationality and utility of your position, you need to reassess your estimation of the success of the project. If you conclude that the limitations placed on you and the project are likely to cause failure, ask yourself whether you wish to be associated with this particular losing project. Essentially, assume that you are not likely to change her mind at some later date. Adjust your expectations accordingly.

Interestingly enough, your client's sense that you might view her position as detrimental enough to cause you to refuse the project may, in itself, change her mind. Never, however, use this as a tactic. If you don't mean to walk away from the project, don't threaten. In fact, don't threaten at all. Merely make clear that, in your opinion, the project cannot be done properly or successfully without greater information sharing and that, therefore, there is little point in continuing.

As you can see, your information needs reach far beyond the standard need for project-related data. You need to have the information that will permit you to be sensitive to the specific people or groups of employees who relate to your project tasks. You need to understand the orientations, styles, and prejudices of the owner/manager/client. In short, you need to have your antennae out at all times and to put together profiles of the company and of key employees much as I suggested in the last chapter you do with potential clients. Updating these profiles as the situation, the people, and their relevant relationships shift over time and with new information is vital to producing successful end products for smaller companies.

Client

Your client may well be nervous about the project he has asked you to do. He is concerned about its success. He is concerned about what the solution is likely to require of him. He is concerned that you will find he did something wrong and that you will think poorly of him (or, worse yet, tell someone). He is concerned that his problem might be unsolvable or terminal for the company.

Most of these concerns are common, to one degree or another, to all consulting clients. Smaller company clients, however, respond to these concerns on two levels. While an executive of a larger company is involved on the business level, a smaller company owner/ manager is also very personally involved. The company is *his* company in a very different way. He built it (or his father built it). His children will inherit it. He and the company are identified with one another. Thus, your probing in the company may elicit the personal-level reactions generally reserved for doctors.

You will not be able to change this. There is no real reason to try (unless, of course, your professional work involves owner attitudes and styles directly). What you can and should do is to cope effectively and efficiently with the concerns of your client so you can get your work done properly and with minimum distraction. You can do this by developing and maintaining adequate information flows that address the underlying concerns of your client.

In larger companies, consultants generally report to management clients after rather extended periods of work. Higher-ups typically only want to see fairly solid results. They want to hear about major problems or issues, but they are generally willing to let consultants work independently with whomever in the company it makes sense to work with. In short, information flows tend to be structured and rather formal at the top.

Because of the personal-level concerns of smaller-company owners, however, it is wise to develop and schedule many informal feedback sessions. These can be general updates of progress and/or merely rap sessions. The key idea, though, is to address, directly or indirectly, the underlying client concerns. Thus, such sessions should include reassurances about the solvability of the problem (assuming, of course, you believe it solvable), about past steps taken (unless they created an impending disaster), and about your performance against your budget estimates. While not all of these need to be raised every time, your general approach to discussions with your client should always take such concerns into account.

Since you are aware of the intense and different level of concern on the part of the owner of a smaller company, your client should never have to hunt you down to get answers to questions relating to her project. Your time should be structured to facilitate frequent (daily?) talks, however brief, with her. This offers her the opportunity to raise specific questions with you and also lets her see that you are really there and making progress. You also appear extremely responsive to her needs—a very attractive characteristic in a smaller-company consultant. As an extra added attraction, you get to hear any new information that might bear on your work. Everybody wins. Just remember to include the time for such extended hand holding in your project cost estimates.

NEED FOR CONSENSUS

The open approach to information collection and dissemination also offers additional benefits to consultants and clients in smaller companies. If all concerned know what is going on as it is developing, you will find out rather quickly whether you are likely to have difficulty selling your solutions or recommendations. While attention to acceptance is critical to the success of any consulting project in any company, in smaller companies, lack of appropriate acceptance and support can be fatal more quickly.

An instance from my own experience describes a project that died before it began. And I should have known better.

A small real estate leasing and management company asked me to come in to discuss setting up information management methods and to perform some general organizational and information flow work. The company included the owner, his son, a long-time secretarial/clerical employee, and three full-time employees of shorter tenure. The son, a former student of mine, had called. It seemed that the owner had the physical records of virtually all deals and ownership in three or four different locations, each containing numerous boxes. While he could carry the relevant information around in his head, the other employees had little or no access. They found themselves doing things twice (or more) and sometimes giving their lessees, potential sellers, and potential buyers conflicting information.

As we talked, it became clear that the son was the one who really wanted to organize. The other employees appeared to care little one way or the other. The owner was skeptical, at best. He was the one who would have to spend time on the old records. Better organization would also possibly impair his role as the only one with the relevant information—the one people had to come to for help.

I spent time with them. I described my approach and the process. Other business necessities intervened for them. We talked further. We got to the LOU stage. I sent them the initial items we would work with. I heard nothing. I called. It seemed that some deal was blowing up and we would have to delay just a bit. Delay followed delay until it became clear that the great reorganization was never going to happen.

While one might argue that the fault lay with them, the real problem was that I thought I had appropriate support when I did not. I knew that there was disagreement between father and son—and I went ahead anyway. I had bought the outer trappings of a collegial company while the company was really more a one-man show. I had bet that the son would create accord on the need for the project. I wasted my time (and theirs) because I lost sight of two primary tenets of working with smaller companies:

1. Never try to buck the real power sources in a smaller company.
2. Pay strict attention to *actions* that illuminate the owner's management style rather than the words that describe it.

I only hope that our lengthy initial discussions were of some value to them. That way, at least *somebody* will have gotten something of value from that fiasco—other than my reminder that I should never forget the basics.

This project-that-wasn't is paradigmatic of situations that obtain in many smaller companies. The clear issue is the composition of the consensus required to let a project succeed (or even start). In smaller companies these particular waters tend to be both clearer and muddier, as noted in Chapter 1. There are fewer players to be concerned with. On the other hand, their relationships are likely to be older and, hence, quite likely better submerged or covered. In family-owned companies, further complications often occur through various nonbusiness issues and nonblood relationships.

There are two critical issues here for the consultant outsider who wants his project to succeed. First, he must determine where the real power lies in the company. Second, he must figure out who else will have major influence on any decisions relating to his project. Only after these issues are nailed down can he proceed to build a relevant and useful consensus for his solutions and recommendations.

Who's Really in Charge Here?

As demonstrated, it can be vital to figure out rapidly who is really running the company in which you are about to operate. If for no other reason, you need to know to whom to direct your reports. Of course, you will report to the specific person who signed the contract or accepted your LOU. The issue is rather who *else*, if anyone, is supposed to be on the inside of your project. And *that* sometimes takes some figuring.

The rather irreverent identifiers I assign in the following discussion reflect my personal shorthand for common company approaches to handling internal decision-making responsibilities. While each company is individual, most will exhibit, predominantly, the major characteristics of a single group. Whether you choose to adopt my shorthand is immaterial. The idea is to become able to identify rapidly the general patterns of operation, to structure your project reporting and feedback appropriately, and to build the appropriate consensus for getting the broader job done well.

The "one-man show" is the classic small business image. The owner is founder or his direct descendant. He (or she, though it is less likely) assumes that he *is* the business. He is the only one who can speak for it and the only one who can give it direction. In fact, he generally likes it best if his is the only voice in the place. It usually is after a while—even if it really didn't begin that way.

As long as you do not have to work for him directly all the time, if the one-man showman is genial and smart, it is relatively easy to overlook his arrogance. If you choose to do a project in his company, you will report *only* to him. If you disagree with him, it is wise to couch your disagreements carefully. And give him lots of time to change his mind. When he does so, he will have figured it out all by himself. If this will be a problem for you, stay out of one-man shows.

Two different types are at the far other end of the scale. The first is the company that is "just one big happy family." It lives on complete consensus. These are usually very small companies (nothing would get done otherwise). Everybody has a vote and most votes are equal. While it sounds like these would be good companies to work with, in reality, they are extremely frustrating because nobody can make a decision. You report to everyone and are, in a sense, answerable to everyone.

Only slightly better are the "vote takers." In these companies, most employees have a vote, but it is generally clear that the owner (or at least one specific person) makes the final decision. She usually does so by majority rule or on the basis of some kind of vote-weighting system. For the outsider, the tricks are to determine who the voters are and, even more important, to figure out the vote-weighting system as it relates to the project in question.

Companies run by "coaching crews" are similar in many respects to the two types just described. The difference is in the distribution of the votes. Coaching staff companies have relatively few employees with votes. The type has two main variants that are roughly equivalent to the preceding two. Those with clear head coaches have the advantage of having someone definitely in leadership roles. Those without head coaches are likely to flounder when it comes to decision time. When doing a consulting project for a coaching crew company, the consensus you require will be among the coaching staff. You want, in particular, the head coach, if any.

Coaching crew companies are frequently partnerships in which all partners work in the business. They are often second- or third-generation family businesses in which various branches of the family have operating ties to the business. Such ownership or familial issues often intensify differences about basic business methods, further complicating your professional work in the company.

In "stalking horse" companies (which also can be thought of as "the man behind the throne" companies), a consultant is at an almost impossible disadvantage because he cannot even talk to the person or people whose agreement is really needed. In effect, your recommendations and solutions will be filtered through whoever is ostensibly making decisions to those who really are. You cannot control the content or the implications directly. You cannot even reasonably demand to see the real decision maker without completely undermining the company "leader" and turning him entirely against you. These projects will truly try your patience and fortitude.

"Stalking horse" companies may be companies in which the founder is legend. Though "The Old Man" is still alive, he doesn't come to the office or plant any more. People ostensibly running the show, however, are likely to refer to him frequently in talking with you. They may feel (or actually be) compelled to clear all major decisions with him. "The Old Man" may also be "Mother" (usually the founder's wife who took over when "The Old Man" died and who ran the company for years) or a major family shareholder who doesn't work in the company—the president's wife or the chairman's daughter. The major fact about this person (or these people) is that, although they really run the show, they are not there.

In short, although smaller companies are made up of fewer individuals than larger companies, small company relationships, as they relate to the work of professional consultants, can be more byzantine. As I relearned at that real estate company, a consultant's first task is to assess the power structure and personalities in the company with which she is contemplating involvement. These relationships define the kind(s) of agreement that will be needed to perform project work properly and to get results implemented. In recognizing and working with the relationships lies the ultimate success of your smaller company consulting project.

Getting Everyone Going in the Same Direction

Once you determine who you need to convince—to sell, if you will—you need to determine how to do it within the confines of your particular project. As noted earlier, my personal preference is to run completely open projects. Under those rules, you simply make all information and all arguments available to all relevant people. As also noted earlier, this is not always feasible. Nor is it always simple.

A word of caution is critical here: Nothing in this (or any other) section should be read to mean that you should create different stories and/or different facts or findings for different people. Aside from the ethical issues raised by that method of operation, in smaller companies even people who are at odds on virtually everything talk with one another. There's nobody else to talk with. Your project is a likely discussion topic. If you sing different songs, you are quite likely to be found out. Then, however good your actual work, you are through. Your departure might become the one issue in thirty years on which two parties have agreed.

Despite the foregoing caution, it is not necessary to use the same *emphasis* and *perspective* in all your discussions with relevant company personnel. As you know, where you stand depends on where you sit. Thus, the value your work offers to one department head may be different from the benefit viewed by another. Thus, as you develop your recommendations, consider them from the perspectives of the relevant players in your game. How will this make John's life easier? How will it speed the work in Alice's shop? Essentially, the goal is to sell the particular benefits of your recommendations to the beneficiary—without shifting your basic ground.

You also should not minimize any significant difficulties. It is a rare manager who cannot instantaneously find the problems—particularly if he doesn't want to deal with your results. You thus gain nothing and lose a great deal by pretending the difficulties don't exist. You win by having seen them and offering ways around them or approaches to them. Sympathizing and offering assistance also helps. And continue to sell the basic benefits.

In addition to building consensus for your project recommendations, you have still another task in maintaining communications within your client company. It is your job to keep the original focus of the project. In smaller companies, this tends to be more difficult than it is in larger companies for two main reasons:

1. Managers in smaller companies tend to be responsible for broader areas of operation than their larger-company counterparts.
2. Particularly in non-one-man-shows, managers in smaller companies tend to believe themselves part of the company as a whole rather than the representative of a division or specific discipline.

Taken together, these two factors mean that everybody will have an opinion regarding what you are about. Each opinion will differ from all the others. Guaranteed.

The trick for the consultant is not to get seduced by these varying visions of what his work is supposed to be about. This can be done only by maintaining the focus on the project definition you developed with your client at the outset. The one you wrote up in your LOU. Because everything is connected to everything else in an operating company, the real danger of losing the specific, narrow focus that you and the owner defined is that you will end up being responsible for a much enlarged project for which you cannot collect an adequate amount of money. After all, the new, redefined, larger project is *not* what the owner agreed to.

Monetary issues aside, expanding the project on an ad hoc basis in response to the definitions of other managers leaves you extremely vulnerable to getting nothing done at all and scattering your resources (which, I assume, are limited). At best, the work that your owner-client wants done will get shorter shrift, about which he is likely to be displeased. At worst, you will have been sucked into addressing issues that your owner-client specifically does *not* want to address. You will have become a playing piece in someone else's game (see Chapter 2).

Maintaining the focus is *your* job, since you are the likely major loser if you fail to do so. This needs to be done gently, particularly in companies with various kinds of voting-bloc decision-making methods. The least personal way to maintain your focus is to use your LOU project definition as your fixed, short-term job description. You point to it as the only thing that will be permitted by the owner. It essentially ties your hands. Though you would really love to help out, you really cannot. You are very sorry.

If you think the proposed expansion is a good idea, you might suggest that the manager/partner/other who is interested propose a specific expansion to your owner-client. That way, if you become responsible for it, you can, at least, negotiate its terms and provide for its expenditures in time and money. It would become a formal, defined part of your project rather than something you became responsible for almost by accident.

GETTING YOUR HANDS DIRTY

Perhaps one of the most interesting differences between larger and smaller companies lies in the way they view expertise—particularly consulting expertise. In a smaller company, despite the fact that you are an expert, you are likely to be expected to get your hands dirty, to prove your expertise on the shop floor. In most larger companies, expertise is permitted to exist with clean hands. In short, in a smaller company, there will be not one question but two. Owners and other personnel will want to know not only whether you know anything but also whether you can actually *do* anything. It is wise to take this into account as you present your expertise to smaller companies.

Reasons for this difference can be found in the structure and scale of most smaller enterprises. First, the owner, and most key staff people, probably began by doing everything in the company themselves. "Everything" most likely included sweeping the floors and fixing the equipment. You, as "expert," should, therefore, know better than they how to sweep the floor or fix the machines.

In short, the notion of what expertise is all about is essentially different in smaller companies from the concept in larger ones. The concept of specialization, while understood on an intellectual level, is not highly integrated into the expectations of owners of smaller companies. You, by contrast, as a consulting expert, live on the concept of specialization. You need to be aware that your smaller company clients view a specialty more broadly than you do. The ways in which you demonstrate and validate your expertise must take this into account. It will not do, for example, to announce your expertise. Those who are buying it must be convinced that it exists or they will neither buy nor cooperate in your project. Convincing may involve demonstrations and/or a parade of concrete results.

This difference in definition of expertise is coupled with a deep distrust of folks who talk a lot but cannot (or do not) *do* anything. Consultants (not you, of course, but most consultants) are known for talking a better game than they actually play. For the smaller-company owner, a practical orientation will take precedence over theory, writing, or other nonproductive activity. After you describe your project to a small-company owner or management group, for example, prepare for questions such as, "What were the results the last three times you did this?" or "How did that work in real life?" If you cannot answer clearly and in the practical spirit of the questions, you are likely not to be able to make the project work.

Happily, the second major reason for the smaller-company bias toward getting one's hands dirty offers a simple vehicle for showing your willingness and ability to do just that. Most smaller companies are perennially short of staff. Thus, everyone is expected to pitch in on anything when the need arises. When a consultant, the big expert, actually pitches in to help finish some job, he really impresses the troops, and the managers. What impresses is not only the willingness and ability but also the commitment that is read into the gesture by the other workers. You can count it as a big win for your side.

Opportunities for such activities abound in most smaller companies. I have sat down at a typewriter when it made sense to do so (to great surprise and much giggling from the secretaries, especially when they saw my skill level). I have helped assemble various contraptions. I have helped move furniture. I demur only when I am likely to wreck the final product. This is generally good policy—good for your reputation with clients and for relationships within the client company.

Federal Express, a specialist of a sort, gained a smaller-company client for life through just such pitching in. The company was getting out a major shipment of bound materials. They arranged for the last Federal Express pickup on the way to the airport. Two couriers arrived at about nine o'clock. The material was not ready. Those two guys could have stood around sipping coffee or rushing the customer. Instead, they looked at their watches, announced that they absolutely had to leave by 9:30, and began helping to bind, staple, and pack the books. The shipment made the plane. The owner has not yet stopped talking about the incident. It cost Federal Express nothing extra. Their two people would have had to stay anyway.

So get your hands dirty. Playing standoffish expert is generally not the best role for a smaller-company consultant. Ivory towers don't sell well in this segment.

YOUR MANY ROLES

As you can see from the previous discussion, people who are successful consultants to smaller companies play numerous, often highly varied roles in their client companies. Given the sizes of the companies, you are likely to be interacting with people from more layers of a company, with a greater variety of skill levels, and with people who come from more varied backgrounds than you would in a larger company. In my view, this is one of the things that makes working with smaller companies particularly enjoyable and rewarding. It also makes it more complex. You cannot simply make your expert pronouncements and leave. You wind up both giving and getting more.

In addition to your role as expert, in smaller companies you will also be called upon to play teacher, leader, and cheerleader. Sometimes, you will find yourself playing all these roles, each with different groups in the company. Sometimes, you will get to do all of them at once. That's when the act gets interesting.

This section outlines these various roles and discusses briefly when and with whom they tend to be most useful. None of them (including your primary role as expert) will work, however, unless there is some measure of sincerity and honesty behind your words and actions. People in smaller companies generally have extremely sensitive garbage detectors. And they react very negatively to people who play games with them. Thus, you need to view the playing of these various roles not as a big game but rather as the best, most efficient, and most effective means of assisting your client and her staff to deal with the issue(s) you have been brought in to address.

Leader

As was intimated in the preceding section, one of your major roles is as project leader. Whether or not there is a project leader on the client staff for this project, you are essentially the one who is responsible for the ultimate success of the project. This is as it should be, since although the client will have to live with the project results, so will you. To the extent that a consultant is really only as good as his last job, your reputation may be more at risk than anything in the client company. There is nothing as good as a really good consultant disaster story. If the project fails (or does not succeed enough) your client at least gets one of those stories. It will get even better (more disastrous to your reputation) in the retelling.

As leader, it is your job to keep everyone on track toward the goal(s) of your project. You can use the methods outlined earlier or anything else that may work. You must see to it that resources are committed as needed and as promised by the owner and/or staff members. You must work with client schedules so that your project gets done on its schedule without disrupting all the other schedules in the shop.

The process of ensuring that your project gets done on time and at budget will probably require that you take on parts of various other roles. You may need to become a diplomat, negotiating compromises on schedules or staffing needs. You may need to become peacemaker between warring groups or departments, both of which you need to get your work done. You will almost surely need to be part juggler, keeping everyone's scheduling and staff needs up in the air at the same time. It will be unacceptable to produce no results or late results because you could not provide the leadership required to resolve these normal difficulties in the process of a consulting project.

Your role as leader is likely to be required at all levels of the company. Yet you must be careful about usurping the broader leadership role of the owner, president, or head coach. My personal approach is to make continuous political assessments of which leadership pieces relate only to this project and which would be in the longer-term leadership interest of the owner (my client). In those places where the longer term is involved, I try to ensure that the owner and I work in tandem or, better still, that the owner alone is viewed as the leader. While this means I take a temporary back seat, my clients appreciate the courtesy and the clear understanding of the essential difference in our two roles. It allays a common early fear that the expert will displace the owner in the regard of the staff. This makes for good client relations and, in the longer run, more and better business.

Cheerleader

As the project progresses, you will often find a cheerleader role required. Particularly in longer projects, it is difficult for everyone, especially those in subordinate positions, to see any progress. Eventually, it becomes difficult for most personnel to *care* whether there is any progress. If you are planning to bring your project to a successful conclusion, you have to find ways of reviving flagging interest and enthusiasm.

While both major ways of rekindling the flame are rather obvious, as a project progresses, you, too, will probably lose your initial enthusiasm. Middles of projects are generally things to be gotten through. This review can serve to remind you of what you have to do whether you feel like it or not.

The first cheerleader operation is to remind the relevant people of how far they have come already. This is a standard variant on getting people to see the doughnut rather than the hole or the half-full glass rather than the half-empty one. This process accomplishes two goals. First, it gives the troops a feeling of accomplishment, which is usually sorely needed in the middle of a project. Second, it minimizes the hassles yet to come, if only by contrast.

Group review sessions are convenient times to play this role. While not forgetting what still needs to be done and what is behind or not progressing as smoothly as it should, you can emphasize group triumphs and the various positive things that have already flowed from the project. If one department or one person has done something outstanding on the project, this is also a good time to let everyone know about it (unless, of course, he is the most hated guy in the whole company already). Although they are not your people forever, they are who you have to work with to bring this particular project in. You need to motivate and work with them using everything you know.

A second classic motivating/cheerleading device is the well-deserved pat on the back. Most of us tend to scream loudly when things are not done right or when they are not done on time. Few, however, really recognize work that is there when it is supposed to be and is of the quality that you need.

In a consulting situation, client people are likely to be working with you as an add-on to their regular work. Getting something to you on time is often a minor miracle. Not to recognize that, even if only

by a sincere thank you and a comment to the effect that you understand how hard it was to do, is *de*motivating. Keep firmly fixed in
mind that those folks do *not* work for you. You will win or lose,
however, largely because of them.

Cheerleading is also often useful with your actual client. She was
hesitant about calling you. She may have had all those concerns discussed earlier. Describing progress—particularly in terms of how
good it was that she caught the situation so early in its development,
etc.—can go a long way toward calming her fears and helping her to
feel good about her decision.

Oddly enough, playing cheerleader for others often helps *you*
get back into project work. You needn't see it as entirely selfless.

Obviously, *do not make the cheers up out of whole cloth.* Your
audience will know you are lying. You will be viewed with distrust
and probably with distaste. (And your project will probably suffer.)
But given an opportunity to cheer, do so with enthusiasm. Given a
group win, celebrate. It not only makes working together easier but
also makes finishing successfully more likely.

Teacher

Discussing the teaching role of a consultant to smaller companies moves us immediately back into the realm of strategy and
underlying objectives. Thus, this section reflects a very personal view
of what my practice is really all about.

In my view, my role as teacher is the most important one I can
play in a smaller company. While my project will do something useful
for the company (or I wouldn't have taken it on), the more lasting
contribution that I can make to that company is to leave it better able
to operate without me and without other consultants. This is essentially a teaching approach: "Give a man a fish and he will eat a meal.
Teach him how to fish and he will always be able to eat."

Teaching is frequently viewed as dry and exceedingly annoying
to the objects of the lessons. I am convinced that this need not be the
case. I think most of my clients and even most of my former students
would agree. The issue is how and why the teaching/learning occurs.

The teaching/learning process in a smaller-company consulting
project should grow naturally out of what is going on in your project
and be coupled with the natural curiosity of most people. Essentially,
you are there doing new things (or old things in a new way). People

will be interested. Teaching can be as simple as describing what you are doing and why as you go about it. Learning occurs almost by accident as those with whom you are working work with you. The dryness and boredom only occur when you are teaching "at" someone who is essentially not involved.

At another level, the teaching role should be built into the structure of a project. I try, for example, to provide for meetings at which the reasons for doing things are explained or the methods are discussed. While I am hardly enamored of meetings, I recognize that I cannot implement a project in someone else's company. Only the client and his staff can do that. I am responsible for showing them why they should care enough to bother to do it.

I also try to structure time into a project for developing training materials and methods, if necessary, and/or for holding training sessions before project end. In both these instances, people are unlikely to be turned off because they become (and, unlike you, will continue to be) part of the process. They, after all, will have to take over when you are gone. I view a large part of my job as being to make that transition as painless as possible.

The level of my interest in the teaching role is personal and strategic. A successful consultant in smaller companies must do some teaching, however, if only to ensure the completion of the project. Although you may not view your ultimate objective as making yourself unnecessary, you still have only the client's staff and the client as the means of implementing your project. Thus, in a very immediate sense, your future rests with them. While I probably wouldn't tell them so, I would keep it very much in mind as I worked with them and prepared them to take over.

6

THE CONSULTING PROCESS: IDENTIFYING PROBLEMS AND MAKING RECOMMENDATIONS

Very often you will find that, despite a clear statement from your client about what the problem is, that isn't what the problem is. You have, however, agreed or contracted to solve the problem. This leaves you with two tasks rather than the one you thought you had. You first have to figure out what the problem is. Only then can you figure out how to solve it.

This chapter is designed to help you in two ways. First, it outlines a number of the most common underlying difficulties that occur in smaller companies. This should assist in targeting major problem areas for you. Second, it offers an approach to addressing these problem areas: defining the particular problem(s) you find and developing your recommended solutions.

Since you know your professional field better than I know it (I hope), there is no useful way I can help you *solve* the problems you find. However, to the extent that the key to problem solving is determining the right problem to solve, this chapter can help. Nobody ever built a good consulting reputation or a large consulting practice on solving, however brilliantly, the wrong problems.

UNDERLYING DIFFICULTIES OF MANY SMALLER COMPANIES

There are two approaches to getting a grasp on the broad problem areas that appear to affect smaller companies most and most frequently. One is statistical. A second deals with the orientations of most owners of smaller companies. In discussing both, my objective is to let you see the thought and activity patterns that such owners often follow in getting their businesses into the kinds of trouble they have called you to get them out of. Using this information in conjuction with the information that your client (or prospective client) has given you about the specifics of his company and his problem, you will be better equipped to target the broad dimensions of the issue. Later, I offer a useful technique for refining problem definitions.

Probabilities

The quickest way to see what problems constitute the bulk of serious small-company problems is to examine what finally brings smaller companies down. Dun & Bradstreet (D&B) compiles and publishes just such information about why businesses fail. They survey failed firms and report on the reasons at two levels. Since the reasons and the proportional distributions of the reasons have remained rather stable over time, these problem areas can be viewed as critical for smaller companies.

In very general terms, the failure factors defined by D&B involve one or more difficulties in handling money, markets, and management. The first-level list shows that most failures result from inexperience and/or incompetence (92.1 percent in 1980). This figure simply highlights something you already know: that companies that do not know enough to call for knowledgeable help when they need it (or do not call even if they know) get into real trouble.

The more interesting issues arise from D&B's second-level lists. Such lists break down the inexperience/incompetence category into the various areas in which it is apparently most dangerous to be inexperienced and/or incompetent. One such list looked as follows:

Inadequate sales	49.9 percent
Competitive weakness	25.3

Heavy operating expenses	13.0
Receivables difficulties	8.3
Inventory difficulties	7.7
Excessive fixed assets	3.2
Poor location	2.7

There are two clear limitations to the use of this list as a direct tool by a working consultant. First, the source of the data is heavily oriented to financial reasons for failure. While financial terms are generally the ones that define *failure*, this orientation limits the usefulness of the data for consultants who work outside the strictly business areas. Second, even for those consultants who work in related areas, the list remains far too general to offer solid working hypotheses for an individual company.

The advantage of knowing this information—for any consultant to smaller companies—lies in two areas: (1) It can help increase your ability to assess the severity of a problem in a client company, and (2) it can alert you to real problems that might underlie the problem the owner thinks he has and that he has told you about.

An example might illustrate this process. I recall an owner who wanted to talk with me about his difficulties in raising money for his new company. He wanted to raise funds without giving up too much ownership (a perfectly reasonable goal, if sometimes difficult to accomplish). The only alternative he saw was to borrow the large sum of money. Happily, he recognized the very heavy burden that such borrowing would place on the new company. He also harbored some doubts about whether the company would be able to borrow as much as he thought he needed.

My first question was whether he really needed the money at all, remembering that excessive investment in fixed assets and inventory often sinks companies. In fact, when we explored his situation, it transpired that he could defer raising money without damage to his plans. (When he *does* need to raise money, he will get a better deal because his company will be more established.)

This is a clear case of talking yourself out of a job. I passed up the chance to do massive financial analyses and to make presentations to investors and bankers on behalf of this owner. His company will be better for my noninvolvement. I banked on my belief that owners of smaller companies tend not to forget those who do them good turns. If I am correct, I should see numerous referrals from this owner—and have the opportunity to do his financing when the time is riper. (If I am wrong, I blew a day of my time.)

As you can see, the primary value of the list of very general failure factors lies in its springboard potential. Using it, a consultant can see very clearly the potential consequences of various types and levels of smaller-company difficulties. In fact, a good way for you to begin to incorporate awareness of these failure factors into your consulting approach would be to define relationships between your particular field and relevant factors.

Try sitting down with the list, considering each factor alone, and determining which issues raised in your kind of practice might or do impinge upon the factor being considered. If, for example, you deal in management styles, you might consider, say, how the "edifice complexes" of many owners relate to both their management styles and to the longer-term health of their companies. If your owners have difficulty in motivating or communicating with employees (or have twice as many people as they really need), consider how those issues might contribute to such potentially terminal problems as inadequate sales or heavy operating expenses.

In short, many smaller companies operate rather close to the edge. As a consultant to such companies, part of your job is relating whatever you are doing to the survival and prosperity of the company. The more you know about what kills companies, the more effectively you can do this.

Personalities

Some of the more common issues that arise in the personalities of owners and managers of smaller companies have been noted in passing earlier. In this section, therefore, these foibles are treated briefly. The real business of this section is to consider some of the underlying reasons or tendencies that produce some of the more spectacular examples of the behavior of owners of smaller companies.

Briefly, these kinds of behaviors are generally those of extremes. One owner will not spend a nickel on any equipment that is new and not absolutely necessary (*necessary* being defined as replacing a machine built in 1920 that is in pieces on the shop floor). Another likes gadgets and picks up any new gear that is impressive and might work in her company. One overworks personnel, who are spread so thin that any glitch in the system means that things will start falling through ever-widening cracks. Another likes multitudes of people crying "Yes, Sir!" in unison, so he hires more people than he could ever use profitably.

As you can surmise, this kind of behavior results from two major factors. First, there is the ownership argument: I built it; I own it; I can mess it up if I want. There is nothing that can be done for an owner of this sort. He doesn't want your advice anyway. He has probably hired you either to agree with his conclusions or to do some production-type job. If you have a great deal of patience and an equal amount of free time, you might try to make a convert to reasonableness, but be prepared to write off the effort.

The second factor originates in uncertainty and lack of knowledge. People are often most vociferous in condemning that about which they feel insecure, uncomfortable, or untutored. You can deal with this factor. There are two underlying types of such behavior. Each can have many variations on the same theme. Since they are so common, a brief discussion of some of the major variants might be useful.

Planning. This is a big issue in smaller companies. Most owners do not see any reason for formal planning of any type. Some academic types, in essence, agree with them, building nonformal planning models and arguing for nonplanning planning. I (and you, as well, no doubt), however, get to see firsthand the results of constant-surprises management. We get to try to keep the pieces together (or put them back together). We know that constant-surprises management can be terminal.

It is almost understandable that owners of smaller companies do not want to look and/or plan ahead. They see a world of giants in which they are highly vulnerable. They see sweeping economic forces over which they have no control. They see competitors who would love to get their hands on company planning documents. In short, they see hostility out there. Some see this hostility as directed against them or against small creatures in general. Others see it as highly impersonal. But it's out there.

What is interesting is the common reaction of not looking—almost as if it will go away if you don't notice it. Or perhaps it can't see you if you are not looking at it. Numerous former owners will attest that it will *not* go away, nor will it fail to see someone who is not looking. In fact, there are those who assert that "it" particularly enjoys taking the unwary by surprise.

The other end of this spectrum includes the owner who is absolutely confident that it doesn't *matter* what the rest of the world is like. He appears to believe that the sheer force of his personality, the beauty of his product or concept, or pure unfounded goodness will ensure that his company will survive. These are generally owners in the "I can do anything I want" group.

Yet another classic reason for avoiding planning is the claim that "I have no time." In a sense, of course, not planning virtually guarantees that an owner will have no time. She will wind up fighting a continual series of "fires" that are experienced as emergencies or as crash-and-burn programs simply because they were not planned for. Many of these fires arise from foreseeable events and, hence, can be dealt with in advance.

A story told me by a banker leads the field of classic nonplanning stories. The owner of a small, successful manufacturing company called his banker in an absolute panic one Thursday night. He had just discovered that he hadn't enough cash to cover the morning's payroll. Could the banker please make him a (very) quick loan? Needless to say, the banker couldn't. The problem was less the creditworthiness of the company than the management methods of the owner.

Perhaps the real reason that planning is so little done in smaller companies is simply that most owners do not know how to do it in ways that will make the process and the results effective in their companies. As you work with your smaller company clients, then, two things might make your life (and eventually theirs) easier. First, keep track of areas in which some kind of planning process might assist in the longer-term management of the company. Second, work with your client and his people to initiate them into the value of some kind of tailored planning methods.

While this may sound as if you are talking yourself out of yet another job by giving away general planning advice, consider the idea that most clients who do not already plan do not know how to plan. Your existing involvement with the company provides you with both insight into the company's particular problems and needs and some measure of trust from the owner. Who better to assist in developing a targeted, custom approach or method? You may, in fact, wind up with significant levels of follow-on work to your original project.

Once an owner expresses even a modicum of interest in discussing planning matters in your field, a critical trick is to keep away from the technical aspects of the process that are probably what turn you on. Keep the focus on *simple* methods of tracking only key items or issues. Keep the scope of the initial effort as small as possible while generating value for the client. The objective is to show the client that planning need not be painful or complex and that it can be really useful *to him*.

For most owners, the key attraction to planning is generally a heightened ability to anticipate most of the business problems that are likely to occur, enabling the company to avoid them or to address them in advance. The personal benefits of fewer-surprises management for an owner almost always include fewer sleepless nights and, frequently, more income as well. They often get hooked on planning—which may turn out to be a good deal for you as well.

Sell more or cut operating expenses.   Another key fact about many owners of smaller companies is that they tend to focus on the bottom line. While this is laudable in some areas, it frequently narrows their vision of potential solutions to their difficulties. A great deal of small business literature supports them in their priorities by stressing the annual or, worse, quarterly operating results of smaller companies. While bottom line results are obviously important, you may need to remind your owners that other things also have importance in their longer-term business operations.

What results from a strict operating-results focus is sometimes a classic case of solving the wrong problem. The owner of a service company found that he often did not have enough money at the end of the month to cover his obligations. He called his sales staff together and gave a rousing pep talk on selling greater volumes. They did, and lo and behold!, the problem got worse.

It seems that, unrecognized by the owner, his customer mix was changing. The newer buyers paid more slowly. The more the sales-people sold (to these new customers), the greater the cash drain on the company. The focus on the notion that all sales resulted in money and profit caused this owner not to consider other possible causes of his problem. He was in the classic "We're losing money on every unit, but we'll make it up in volume" situation. His limited view of alternative problem definitions caused him to live with the problem for longer than was really necessary, and those were months of significant worry over meeting payroll and basic expenses.

Essentially, the bottom line orientation tends to cause owners to focus on sales and operating expenses rather than financial structure and the sources and uses of assets—the short-term result, often at the expense of longer-term results. This might show up in a personnel-related area, for example, in the hiring of relatively unskilled workers (because they are less expensive) with the intention of training them. The owner may well minimize (at this point in her decision-making process) the competing demands on her time and resources and gloss over the critical nature of service in her industry.

Both planning problems and narrowness-of-view problems are essentially problem-identification and problem-solving difficulties—the kinds that consultants are often called on to fix. It is thus necessary for you, as a consultant, to be able to take the broader view, to raise the planning issues in the hope of heading off future difficulties, to raise alternative problem definitions and different potential solutions. To the extent that you are offering expertise consulting to the owner of a smaller company, those abilities are really what you are selling.

FINDING AND ADDRESSING THE RIGHT PROBLEM

As you already know, a large part of the task of being a good consultant lies in determining and defining the right problem to solve. This has as a prerequisite a healthy skepticism of what the client tells you is the problem. Research described earlier in this book described some of the deficiencies in the problem assessment and diagnostic skills of owners of smaller companies. The previous section suggested some possible reasons for some of these limitations. This section is designed to assist you in taking the necessary steps from the owner's problem definition to one of your own that is specific and clear enough to facilitate the successful conclusion of your project.

As also noted earlier, my assumption is that you know your business. This implies that, while I can help you by suggesting a generic method for pinpointing and defining problems, I cannot offer solutions—except, of course, if your field happens also to be my field.

I can also alert you to the political and personality issues that you may encounter in your problem-definition phase. While these issues are by no means confined to smaller companies, the size and power structure of such companies may permit them to complicate your work even more than they would in a larger company. Smaller company power structures are small (often unitary, in fact). Thus, you are likely to have to convince the owner and his small group that your definition is better (more useful? easier to address?) than his. You will have no outside help in this process, simply because there is usually no outside power source. Thus, redefining the problem the owner sees is often a delicate process.

"Peeling Onions"

This is the easiest way to think about the approach to problem solving that I have found works virtually 100 percent of the time. What your client sees as the problem is "the onion." If you consider what he has told you, you will probably notice that he has defined a set of symptoms as "the problem." As the handiest physician around, your role is to turn that symptom description into an accurate diagnosis and then to develop, prescribe, and perhaps, implement treatment.

As you know, onions are built in layers. Eventually, if you remove layer after layer, you reach an unpeelable core. That core in our metaphorical onion is the underlying problem that you really need to address so you can treat more than just the symptoms of your client's problem. The way you reach it during a consulting project is through questioning. We can look at an example.

Suppose your client has asked you to look at his sales staff. He has seen wide variations in sales among his salespeople. He believes that many of them are inferior. He wants you to develop a method for weeding out "the lazy so-and-sos" with some measure of fairness and objectivity. The problem he sees, his onion, is poor sales because of inadequate sales staff.

If you accepted his problem definition, your major move might be to look at the sales figures by salesperson, seeking information on such items as number of calls per day, number of calls per sale, and similar information. You would be looking for rational cutoff points that might define adequate sales performance.

If, on the other hand, you choose to consider that the problem might be different or broader, you would approach the problem differently. In addition to collecting the sales productivity data, you might also, for example, collect information on the prospects in each sales territory. You might consider the sales and product training of each salesperson. In short, you would look at other things that might be causing the variation in sales that triggered the owner's problem definition.

Your search/questioning process might look as follows:

WHY IS THERE VARIATION IN SALES PERFORMANCE AMONG SALESPEOPLE?

Potential causes:

Lazy people	Poorly trained people	Division of territories

If this is the cause, what should I be able to find?

Territories:	Equal potential	Equal potential	Different potentials
Training:	Equal	Different	Equal
Number of calls:	Different	Equal	Equal

If I find the above, what's my next question?

Is this a motivation problem?	What might be an effective training method?	How might the division be done more reasonably?

As you can see, the numbers of alternative potential problem definitions and layers of the onion could go well beyond what I have outlined here. You could, for instance, also have considered the effects of the compensation system and/or the efficiency of the production and delivery systems. Also, you would peel farther by considering, for example, *why* there is a motivation problem or *why* the hiring process permits adding unevenly trained people, etc. In essence, however, you will have broadened the view of an existing set of symptoms to consider additional possible solutions and next-level problems. You then set about considering what you should find if one hypothesis is true. You then ask why it might be true. When the whys are exhausted (you are at the core of your particular onion), you can then begin to address and solve the real problem.

You could, of course, have simply built this client a system of minimum sales targets for each salesperson—essentially what he asked for. You might point out that we have succeeded in creating vast complexity out of a very simple problem. Simple views, however, have their flaws. No matter how sophisticated your system of minimums might have been, if your only view of the problem was that some of the salespeople were lazy, your system probably would have been inherently unfair to some staffers. This unfairness would be likely to itself become a problem for the sales staff and thus eventually for your client. Moreover, if the real problem was *not* sheer laziness, the next crop of salespeople would likely show the same pattern. Your client would be faced, again, with the same problem that he asked you to solve. Do you think he'll be happy with your performance?

I have made an assumption here about how you want to operate your consulting practice. I have assumed that you want to assist your client to address the underlying problems in ways that will both solve what she currently sees as the problem *and* prevent future symptoms arising from the same root cause; I have assumed that your view of your job is broader than building a quick fix for your client.

This is largely a strategic issue and, as such, is discussed at greater length in Chapter 10. For here, however, let it suffice to say that I have found that quick fixes, particularly if you do not inform the client that all he is getting is a quick fix, tend to create client dissatisfaction later on. Since my objectives are longer term, my concern has to be with long-term client satisfaction. Quick fixes usually do not fill that bill.

Redefining Your Project

Now that you have determined what the real problem is, you usually have another task before you can get down to the real work of solving it. You need to sell the new problem definition. Essentially, you need to rewrite the problem description contained in your LOU or contract to reflect the reality of what you will really be doing for your client. If you fail to perform this step, your client may sequentially:

1. Not care to deal with the problem as you have defined it,
2. Declare (generally loudly) that you have not done what you and she agreed you would do,
3. Refuse to pay you.

She would, of course, be on firm legal ground, since your written agreement would still carry her original problem definition. She might even have good moral ground for her claim, if you had failed to discuss your new view of the problem and your revised approach to it. To invite this level of hassle over something that is preventable is irrational.

But getting agreement to your redefinition may be easier said than done. As already noted, in smaller companies you are generally dealing with a single power source: the owner. There may be personal reasons for not wanting to look at the problem as you have defined it. In the case outlined here, for example, the owner's son or favorite nephew might have the best sales territory. Defining the problem so the solution involves reorganizing those sales territories might embroil him in a massive family row.

Even more likely is a situation in which your redefinition is likely to expose the owner in some way in which he is reluctant to be exposed. While areas of special personal sensitivity vary from owner to owner, they often include the results of management style or attitudes toward money. Such issues frequently get in the way of appropriate management and operation of a company. Those attitudes and predilections, however, are usually deeply ingrained in people—especially in people strong enough to build companies. They feel threatened, resentful, and often aggressive when you blithely tell them that their real problem lies in one of those areas. They believe you are telling them that *they* are the problem—which, of course, you really are and they really are.

You can generally differentiate situations involving personal issues from those in which the owner simply does not understand your view of the problem or merely disagrees with it. You must differentiate so that you can deal effectively with your project work. Again, differentiating involves listening between the lines, for the words are frequently the same. The other component of telling reaction from disagreement has to do with your analysis of the personal/political situation in the company. Both these techniques have been described before. Applications required for this phase of your work are discussed in the next subsection.

Why Is This Owner Arguing?

When you broach the subject of redefining a project with an owner, some owners will jump right in with reasons why your redefinition is poor. Frequently, these are the ones who are somehow personally invested in either the current definition or in not considering your new definition. While such reactive behavior is a good first clue, it is unwise to conclude immediately that the response masks project-related personal issues. Some owners simply react strongly to any changes in what they thought were fixed patterns or concluded discussions.

With such owners, in particular, it is wise to broach the topic of redefinition obliquely and slowly. If you are proposing a major change in what you plan to do for the client, for example, do not expect to start this afternoon. "Have you considered whether . . . ?" offers your client time to reach your conclusion on her own. It is an opening line for a discussion. "I have concluded . . .", on the other hand, is flat, brooking little discussion and forcing her to accept not only your view but also your ability to override her judgments—a position that most people (let alone most owners of smaller companies) are likely to resent and react to.

How your client deals with the "Have you considered . . .?" gambit will tell you a great deal. If he pauses to examine your suggestion(s) carefully, you probably have merely a job of rational convincing to do. I say "merely" because I assume that you have reached your conclusion(s) for good and sufficient reason and are prepared to make a solid case for your position. This, of course, is the minimum requirement for suggesting project redefinition in any case.

If he steps on your last words in a rush to cut you off at the pass, you may be facing a problem. While some people routinely bristle at *any* change in a plan or program, your client is unlikely to be in this group. Anyone who has started a company or is running a smaller one will be inured to changes in plan. You can and should, therefore, assume that your client is trying to avoid something. As you can see, you lose nothing if this assumption is incorrect, a great deal if you assume the alternative and are wrong.

Your response should be to probe into what, precisely, is being avoided and why. This is clearly delicate work, since if the issues are private and personal, the point of the client's whole game is to keep them that way. You, however, must figure it out and take at least a good shot at helping your client to address what you believe to be the right issues. Again, the recommended method is to ask relatively open-ended questions about where and why the client disagrees with your assessment of the situation. Listen carefully to whether what you are getting back is really responsive to the issues you are raising or merely a smokescreen for "I don't want to."

The first rule is to remain focused *strictly* on the business issues, on how failure to deal with whatever problem you have identified will affect the business. You are *not* particularly interested in his personal issues or considerations. You certainly do not want to find yourself privy to personal or family problems. Not only is it embarrassing, but also the fact that you know such sensitive material will make your client wary of you for a long time. Help your client to maintain that business focus as well.

The second rule is to remain relatively low key throughout the entire proceeding. While you have a stake in the outcome of these discussions, it is far smaller and shorter term than your client's stake. More to the point, you hold no power to determine the outcome other than the power of persuasion. Point out the issues and the probable outcomes; point out how negative they are for the business (and, perhaps, for his position as a businessman); but do not threaten dire consequences. Your client clearly finds the issues threatening enough without your help.

As you continue to discuss the redefinition issues, you will find some areas that clearly motivate your client in each direction. Assuming you are listening between the lines (still), you will begin to get a handle on what is frightening about your redefinition. You will also begin to see what particularly attracts him about your proposed changes. Adjust your arguments to begin to address his fears and emphasize his "hot buttons" (what turns him on about your new approach). Do *not* minimize his fears or make light of them in any way, no matter how ludicrous they may seem to you. That is one of the surer ways to lose this person forever.

If you convince your client to accept your redefinition, do not forget to make the appropriate alterations in your LOU. And make sure she sees and agrees to it. The same is true if your client has required no convincing. The project has been changed in some basic ways, and the documentation should clearly reflect the new understanding of what will occur and what the results will look like.

A final note. If your owner is arguing, you are ahead to start with. Some owners, when threatened, simply refuse to discuss the matter. They may cut off your efforts to raise the relevant issues. They may simply listen to you without expression and not respond. You will be able to do little or nothing with such owners. You have no power other than your persuasive abilities, and you are faced with trying to convince a stone wall to please move about three feet to the east.

Under these circumstances, you have only two real choices. You can abandon the project. Or you can deal with the problem as she sees it. Your theoretical third option—to blithely address the problem as you have redefined it—invites forceable ejection from company premises (since you have signaled your play) or, at very least, no payment for your effrontery. In the end, unless you can convince your nonstonewalling clients to adopt your new problem definition, you have the same three (two-and-a-half?) options. All of these options have been discussed before.

REPORTING—AND GETTING YOUR RECOMMENDATIONS ACCEPTED

For many consultants, reporting is viewed as a royal pain, something one has to do but really shouldn't have to. The frequently mentioned reaction is that once the problem is solved, the fun is over. *Explaining* the solution just goes over old ground. Reporting becomes a boring chore, a clean-up operation. Mopping up is never interesting or fun.

We should all keep in mind, however, that the problem isn't solved until our brilliant solutions are implemented and running smoothly in the client's shop. We need to incorporate better the notion that reporting, making recommendations, and getting them accepted by the client and her staff is part of solving the problem. Adding them to the part we tend to think of as the challenging part— solving the problem—would undoubtedly make all our lives more hassle free.

Actually, even if we cannot quite manage the mental contortions necessary to make reporting challenging and interesting, we can go a long way toward making it relatively painless for both ourselves and our clients. The process starts long before you have a fully developed solution to the problem, when it is still fun to talk about the problem and what you are doing with it.

Bite-Sized Reporting

The general idea is to use your periodic discussions with your client and his staff as mini reporting sessions. This accomplishes a number of ends at once. First, you get to be as enthusiastic about the issues, alternatives, potential solutions, etc., as you wish. You will find that your enthusiasm is contagious. At the same time, you are telegraphing your eventual conclusions. This gets people ready for them before you actually put them down as formal recommendations. Finally, you can use these sessions to read any opposition and to build consensus for the recommendations you know are coming. These aspects have been discussed earlier in this chapter.

You are quite likely to find consensus building easier if done on this kind of ongoing basis than if you wait until everything is in your neatly packaged report. If your material is all in one place in a report and if it is the first time client staff has had a shot at it, you can bet it will be one heck of a shot. People become invested in sniping at the report. It is partly the not-invented-here syndrome and partly a natural reluctance to change the way one has always done it. Nevertheless, as we all know, any report provides ample room for nit-picking.

If, on the other hand, you had been building consensus as you went, client people would have invested more of themselves in the concepts and would be likely to help you sell your recommendations. This not only makes your short-term job of finishing the project easier but also makes it more likely that the recommendations will be implemented more quickly and smoothly. This is an additional benefit of the open-project approach described earlier.

Using this approach to reporting, your final report becomes almost a formality. It presents no information or conclusions that have not already been relayed to relevant client personnel. It makes no startling revelations. Since you will have already explained everything, the report can usually be relatively brief. Some clients will want a report simply as a record of your passage and, perhaps, as a reminder of what went on and what was discovered/determined/recommended. It will hardly be long enough to be boring for you.

This does not mean that no written reporting should be done. People have notoriously short memories, particularly about work that they are not enamored of doing. Written pieces should be there to serve as reminders of what they agreed was a good idea or what they have been asked to accomplish. It does mean, however, that reporting, in most cases, can be done in bite-sized chunks. This tends to be less painful for both parties to the process.

Essentially, whenever you have one of your update/conclusion-sharing sessions with your client and her staff, you should also issue a brief paper. This will update project progress and focus on the items/findings/conclusions you wish to discuss that day. These mini-reports can convey information and conclusions, suggest next steps or client participation, and report in a permanent form. In short, they serve all the purposes of a regular report, with one relevant difference. These mini-reports can add a great deal more persuasive argument than a full-blown final report because they are, after all, not formal. You would be wise to make liberal use of that potential. When you need to produce a formal final report for the project, the mini-reports will double as a first draft of the report. You will not be starting from scratch.

A word of warning is in order, however, for those of you who harbor fond hopes of never putting anything like a report in writing. Consider how open you are leaving yourself to charges of not having done the requisite work. While the primary purpose of a report is to convey findings and recommendations to your client in some minimally permanent form, a report also serves as proof that you did the work for which you are seeking payment. Thus, it is in your best interest to provide both yourself and your client with some measure of documentation of the project work done.

Report-Writing (Very) Basics

Since you will have to (or choose to) put something about your projects in writing, a brief section is included here about how to do it. It is very brief since you have undoubtedly heard all this before. I have added a trick or two that I have found helpful in getting through report writing in the hope that they will work for you, too. In the main, however, think of this section as reminder rather than as exciting new stuff.

To the extent that your smaller-company client tends to focus on results and actions, your reports will have to reflect that focus to assure them fair hearings. Not for you the rambling project progress and activity discussion that characterizes so many consulting reports. Your focus must be crisp, clear and to the point—the point, in these cases, being the specific problem or issue that you were brought in to address. Your smaller-company client is not interested in sheer bulk. He didn't call you to build him a doorstop report or a bookshelf volume. He called you for answers. Your reports must give him answers succinctly and simply.

Simply here does not mean that you should gloss over the existing complexity of the problem(s) or offer no alternatives to your recommended course of action; rather, it means that you should explain those complexities and your client's options in a simple manner. In fact, the ruling principle of all reporting (and all writing, in my opinion) should be KISS: Keep It Simple, Stupid. If you think about your roles as consultant and teacher, in fact, your main purpose is to make the difficult intelligible for people who initially do not understand your field. Think of report writing as an extension of those roles.

Keeping it simple should occur along two major parameters: structure and style. Structurally, you want your written material to make very clear to your readers exactly what you have concluded. This means that rather than leading your reader through your analytic processes to your conclusion (the way they taught you in English classes), you want to take a leaf or two out of the journalists' book: "Tell 'em what you're gonna tell 'em. Tell 'em. Then tell 'em what you told 'em." Start with your conclusions, then work through only the relevant parts of your analysis. Smaller-company owners, in particular, are not interested in the nitty-gritty of your process. They will surely be impatient if you try to take them down every blind alley you had to follow in your investigations.

The relevant parts of your analysis are those that helped you to define and discriminate among the options available. They are relevant not because they helped you to reach your conclusion but because they should help your client to reach a conclusion. While you hope that her conclusion will agree with yours (and your in-report sales job should be geared to help her to your conclusion), part of your job is to give her enough information to disagree with you on a rational basis. It is also your job to give her enough information so that she will feel comfortable with whatever conclusion she reaches. At such times, keep firmly fixed in mind that it is *her* company.

A handy way to test the simplicity and logical structure of your -report is to use the old outline method in inverse form. If you are one of those people who does not start with an outline, it is useful to pull out the first sentence of each paragraph of your report as a sort-of outline. If your first sentences make logical sense on their own and are without irrelevant notions, then you probably have a clear report structure.

Examine carefully each paragraph that begins with a sentence that does not logically flow in your outline. If the paragraph really is not needed, strike it. If the paragraph is important on its own, it probably needs to be better connected to the logical flow of the report. Make the required additions and test the section again.

Within paragraphs, your structure should be similar to the structure of the overall report. Start with the main idea rather than leading up to it and having it as the last sentence in the paragraph. (If your paragraph structure is inverted, your first-sentence outline will have looked really weird.) Owners of smaller companies are frequently even more rushed and less patient than executives in general. They often skim through reports, expecting to be able to get the basic ideas from the summaries and the lead sentences. Since your objective is to get your information and recommendations across, you need to accommodate to this predilection.

A pared-down style and language of your written reports should accompany its pared-down structure. While English class essays rewarded complex sentence structure and flowery wording, your client wants "just the facts, ma'am." Your objective is not to write deathless prose, but to have an idea quickly understood. You really do not know a great deal about your total audience. You do not want to make anyone feel stupid for not understanding your words or your sentences. You do not really know the levels of complexity with which your audience can cope. You certainly do not want to be misunderstood. Therefore, never use a two-bit word when a simple one will suffice. Never use three or four words when one will do as well. (My personal "hit list" includes "in order to" when "to" would do and "on account of" for "because," among others.) In short, KISS.

My own trick for ensuring the simplicity of my reports is to write them for a guy I used to work for. This guy could understand words of one syllable—if you said them slowly. Longer words and complex sentences were touch-and-go. As I read a draft, my constant question is: "Would Al understand this?" (I had a lot of practice in writing reports for good ol' Al.) If he probably wouldn't, it's back to the drawing board for a rewrite. If you don't happen to have an Al in your background, perhaps you remember your brother when he was twelve or fifteen years old. (Studies have shown that most people read at about that level.) Try using him as your imaginary report reader.

If all else fails (or if the report is particularly important to you or your client), try finding a real, live reader. The only qualification for this person is that he or she know absolutely nothing about the topic of the report. If your report can make him or her understand the salient points about what you need to tell your client, then it will fly. If not, it's rewrite time (again).

In case it is not yet obvious, the only way to get through reports is to think of them as real parts of the project. If you use the mini-report approach suggested here, it becomes a means of moving the project forward. Your final report can be thought of as your means of launching your fledgling client into implementation on his own. Considered this way, your final report is your final teaching tool. It should serve to reinforce your recommendations and offer some level of assistance when you are long gone. In this respect, your report provides a means of moving your relationship with your client to a different level. A good final report will help you to end your project properly and appropriately—no mean feat as you will see in the next chapter.

7

FINISHING WITHOUT ENDING

Completing your project work in a client company sounds as if it should be easy. You just present your report (or do your presentation or whatever) and you go. Right? Wrong. Like virtually everything else in the smaller-company consulting business, it's not quite that simple. In fact, completing your project work properly can be one of the more difficult parts of doing the project.

There tend to be three major areas of difficulty in getting out gracefully and well. One is tied to your needs. One is tied to the needs of your client. The third stems from the natures of the problems smaller-company consultants are frequently asked to deal with. This chapter addresses all three areas. Its intention is to alert you to the potential hazards and offer you approaches to avoiding or confronting them.

THE PROJECT YOU JUST COMPLETED AND WANT TO FINISH

Let's set the scene. You have been working with Ed and his company, Generic Manufacturing and Sales Corp., for about nine months. Ed had decided to expand his manufacturing operations into a new product line. Partly because of this new line, and partly because of general company growth and industry shifts, he also wanted to convert his entire sales operation from one based on manufacturers' representatives to one that used only company salespeople. He had also wanted to begin national distribution and open a few export markets, but you convinced him to take things more slowly.

Ed wanted you involved in both parts of his company revamping because he saw the changes as inextricably linked. You agreed to perform, sequentially, the markets studies and initial planning for the new product line and then the planning and restructuring of the sales function. You also agreed to develop the new control methods and systems that would permit Ed to keep track of his new sales staff and to monitor how well his new approaches were working.

You, of course, succeeded brilliantly. Based on your market studies, you recommended changes to the proposed line that will strengthen Generic significantly against competitive products. You assisted with equipment specifications and bid evaluation. You frequently worked into the night, in shirtsleeves, side by side with Ed and his people, to deal with the minor bugs that always attend such undertakings. All the while, you were creating a simple, yet innovative, framework and control system for his new sales staffing approach. In short, you have become an accepted part of the scenery around Ed's shop. Everything is ready. Ed and Generic are ready to go. You are ready to get out.

But wait. In this scenario are seeds of the potential problems a consultant to a smaller company can have in ending a client project. First, the overlapping project segments meant that you were around to deal with issues arising from parts you had already completed. Second, Ed and his people have grown to expect that you will always be around and that you are virtually part of the staff (after all, weren't you there that night at midnight when . . . ?). Finally, neither of these would really be *your* problem, save for the fact that you really liked working with Generic and you see the potential for significant additional work with them in the future—if you play your cards right.

CLIENT DEPENDENCE

If you have been working with a client like Ed and with his staff over a fairly long period of time, it is quite possible that they will come to depend on you. While that is what you want, sort of, you really want such feelings to remain within very circumscribed bounds. You want your clients to have confidence in your abilities and to know that they are available if needed and arranged for. You do *not* want them to be convinced that you are the only one connected with the company who can do some function that is necessary to the ongoing business of the company. Basically, you want to be able to leave without the distinct sense that the company will fall apart without you. Dependence of *that* sort is unhealthy for all of you.

Size-Related Reasons for Dependence

Dependence seems to occur in smaller companies more frequently and with greater intensity than it does in larger ones for a number of reasons. First, in a smaller company everyone is likely to be stretched rather thin to begin with. People tend to do two or three jobs as a matter of routine. If you have been around a lot, you begin to be thought of as another staff person, one who has responsibility, de facto, for your area of expertise or skill. It is expected, unless you and your client are very clear about it, that that area of responsibility has been dropped from the agenda of whomever it used to belong to. Quite naturally, that person is reluctant to take back the altered and now unfamiliar function when you are through revamping it.

The recommended approach to working with smaller company staff members may well contribute to this problem. It was suggested that your general approach should be collegial and relatively familiar. As noted earlier, it works well to smooth your path as you develop and garner support for your project work. If unaltered through the life of your project, however, that attitude invites the assumption that you will always be there. Given this possibility, it may be wise to begin to back off a bit, become a little more formal and expertlike as you reach the end of your work. Become more detached in your manner as your project concludes. And be especially clear about about your temporary role in the operations of the organization.

A second contributing factor to the dependence syndrome in smaller companies is that smaller-company owners tend to be rather lonely. They frequently report that they have nobody with whom they can share their real concerns. While this problem apparently goes with the territory, it is a difficult position in which to find oneself. Then you came along and stayed a while. You were another owner of a small company. You knew what it was like. You were being paid to help out, and, undoubtedly, the owner (your client) found you congenial and easy to talk to. So he talked. A lot.

Now you are leaving and a number of things suddenly occur to the owner. First, he may have some nagging concern about your discretion once he is no longer in control of the situation. Second, he is faced with losing his confidante, with going back to having no one who understands. Both parts can be hard. In addition, while you were around, you probably served as a handy font of useful, small pieces of information and tips. Quite likely, the owner and key staff people would come by with a question or an issue just to chew over with you from time to time. With your departure will go this encyclopedia and/or sounding board. These are hard to come by and difficult or impossible to replace. Your departure will leave a void in what has become normal operations.

In this area your choices are really rather limited. Awareness of what might be going on may help, but you still really have only three methods of dealing with this kind of dependence. First, you might never let it get started in the first place. This involves remaining aloof from your client and key staff and actively discouraging any communications that do not relate directly to the business you are there to do (defined narrowly, of course). As noted earlier, this attitude may well impede your work within the company and may also make it more difficult to have your recommendations accepted or even addressed appropriately. You come out clean but cold and, perhaps, without the warm feelings of success you envisioned when you started. (I find it virtually impossible to assume the required attitudes.)

Second, you can simply let the dependence run its course, understanding that once you are out of there you won't really care and your lack of proximity will help the problem die a normal death. You resign yourself to frequent calls from various staff members on all kinds of odd issues for as long as it takes—or until you've had enough.

This course has a number of drawbacks, not the least of which are hassle and the possibility that you will, some day, have to tell it to them straight. The major drawbacks, however, stem from the fact that these dependence relationships often occur on two levels: personal and business. While both parts can create difficulties in your life, personal involvement is likely to create only personal difficulties. Dealing improperly with business-level dependence can play havoc with your company.

If you had enough patience, you could simply keep collecting personal-level confidantes until you ran out of time in your life. Not recommended, but theoretically possible. On a business level, however, your former client may notice that she is now getting, for the price of a phone call, that for which she used to pay serious money. Obvious question: Why pay more? Equally obvious answer: Don't. Milk the relationship. There goes your possible follow-on business. Your former client may also chuckle gleefully over the notion of hoodwinking you—a picture I find hard to deal with, even in my imagination.

This business-level reaction need not even be consciously grasping to have highly negative effects. Your client may really believe she needs you for something and is calling as an old friend or as a former client. She also undoubtedly believes that it is as if you were in her company offices and her question or issue is really quick. You are not, however. You are in the middle of someone else's project. If you mention, after having answered some of her questions, that information is what you sell for a living, odds are she will feel mortally offended. You will have abruptly changed the rules of the game and become the grasping consultant. You lose anyway.

There is a third way that often works to provide a thin, but walkable, line between being aloof and cold and being so friendly that you acquire hangers-on for life. This middle ground lies in how you handle the questions and issues that arise while you are still in the client company. It requires you to take a teaching/leading role in non-project-related client discussions, using what used to be called the Socratic method of questioning. When it works (which I have found to be frequent), it gets you off most of the dependence hooks but adds one small area that requires caution.

Essentially, in talking with clients *about topics not in your area of expertise,* try to ask more questions than you answer. Your questions should lead them through the thought processes needed to reach the conclusion you reached instantly. This method takes longer, but it offers you two main advantages. If the staffer is merely being lazy, your technique will be more hassle to him than it is worth. Instantly, your nonwork advice/question clientele gets smaller. If the questioner is sincere, using this technique gives him the opportunity to learn the method for arriving at an answer on his own, rather than learning the answer. This method of coping with the advice issue thus becomes a tool for increasing the independence, abilities, and confidence of your client and his staff to address the kinds of issues they bring to you for discussion. You are fostering independence rather than dependence. (A little cheering from the sidelines when the questioner gets it couldn't hurt either.)

You will note that I recommend that you confine this kind of activity to issues outside your field of expertise. *In* your own field, your client has a right to expect answers (assuming that that was part of your agreement). He also probably expects that you will go some distance toward training him and his employees as relevant to your project. You, after all, are there as the expert. Moreover, you do not want him to believe that, since he can reach his own conclusions (which, it is implied, are as good as yours), he doesn't need you at all any longer.

General Reasons for Dependence

The dependence syndrome occurs, though less frequently, in larger companies as well. There, executives have other executives with whom to talk, and employees can generally find others to use as sounding boards. Given that some forms of hanging on to consultants occurs even in that environment, there must be causes other than overcommitment and loneliness. Considering three possible other reasons might be useful as you evaluate dependence problems in your client companies.

Status.   This one is akin to the loneliness issues but generally comes from lower-ranked personnel in a client company. Particularly for an employee who does not seem to fit in the client company, having the expert as a friend can be a very powerful status item. It may be even better when you have gone and your name and the fact that "I was just talking with him" can be dropped in casual conversation. You need to watch this, since frequently providing this kind of service to one employee will alienate several others—including, perhaps, your former and prospective client. This is yet another area in which keeping eyes and ears open and tuned can be important.

Laziness.   It is easier to ask someone than to do the work or thinking yourself. Since there are lazy people out there, you need to develop an ear for differentiating between laziness and real questions. A good clue is the tendency of a lazy person to want just the answer, no explanation, no embellishment. Most people tend to be interested in the whys and hows, even if it takes some effort to understand or grasp them.

Fear. Any company in which you are working is probably undergoing change. Change, for some people, is almost inherently frightening. What better way to minimize the impact than to be close to the change-bringer? This will cause such individuals to gravitate toward you.

Those who fear that they will not be able to handle the changes in methods or procedures will also be in your office or at your desk with increasing frequency as your project draws to a close and you threaten to leave. They will be seeking reassurance or one more lesson in how to do it or advice on how to handle things in case something really improbable should occur. Treat these people gently, if you can. They have real problems that you cannot solve but that you should try not to augment. While you should not spend your life (or massive amounts of your client's time) dealing with this level of dependence, you might alert your client to the need of the person for some extra support.

The real point here is that ending a relatively long project involves changing some patterns that have become accepted in the client company. Radical alterations in pattern are difficult for all people. For your departure to go smoothly (and for your project as a whole to succeed), it is generally wise to plan the progress and completion of your work with these dependence/ independence issues in mind. To my mind, such planning must include assisting client staff in feeling comfortable in whatever revised procedures or processes will result from your project and being available for legitimate project-related questions and issues. (This last is discussed later in the section on maintaining relationships.) It does *not* include keeping in constant contact with client or client staff, and it does *not* include playing psychologist for client and staff. (That is not my field.) I suggest that you consider, in advance, what it includes for you.

HOW FAR TOWARD IMPLEMENTATION?

If you review the Generic Manufacturing scenario, you will see another issue in getting out: When is a project really over? In Ed's case, he has precedent for believing that you will work with the company closely through project implementation. After all, you were around while they implemented the manufacturing part of your project. And you pitched in to help. Has Ed any reason for believing that your second phase should stop short of implementing your personnel system?

Yes, I know that your LOU states clearly that implementation is the responsibility of Generic Manufacturing and Sales. But you implied a change in that when you worked on implementing the product line. And, besides, where does development end and implementation begin? Particularly since the waters have been muddied by the consecutive projects?

And what if your LOU states that you will assist in implementation? When is a project implemented and ready to become part of operations? In reality, neither you nor your client wants you there forever.

As you can see, the essential issues are two. First, when does the project no longer require your services? Second, when have you fairly and properly discharged your responsibility to your client? Sometimes, these issues are really the same issue. Sometimes they are different. To highlight the differences, each is discussed as a separate issue.

Requirements of the Project

Each project is different. Having said that, one must point out that every project also has its own logical imperatives and clear checkpoints. While most of them can be laid out in advance in your LOU, the events and progress of a project may well demand some modifications. The objective is to meet the intent of the LOU rather than the absolute letter thereof.

Suppose, for example, that as you worked with Generic's new personnel methods, it became clear that two kinds of hires were needed and that your system would, therefore, need more extensive testing than you had originally anticipated. While once simple passive testing of the system would suffice as the end point defining "ready to implement," you now believe that some live testing would be a more appropriate definition of the end of your project. The project has effectively redefined its proper end. (You must, of course, clear your new view with Ed, since it will undoubtedly add time to your billings.

He will probably agree since he is by now getting nervous about implementing on his own. If you agreed to a fixed price deal, you have to wrestle with your conscience over the conflict between time and project requirements.)

The idea is to let the project dictate, to some degree, what its end is. This is an analytic process, not an emotional one. The analysis should include what it is about the project that has changed so that it is now necessary to redefine the point of your leave taking. If you cannot find compelling reasons within the project itself for extending your stay, look very carefully at your own motives and feelings about the project, your client, and her company. You may be developing a problem of your own.

The danger is that the reverse of client dependence may occur. Consultants sometimes get so caught up in being the expert, the big cheese, that they have trouble letting go of a project. They may get to like this particular client environment and/or the level of adulation or appreciation they get from the troops. They may also just fall in love with the system, approach, or product they just created. It is also undeniably easier to stay longer than to develop new business and face new uncertainties. The project then begins to whisper, "Stay, stay" in their ears. They become convinced that the client and her staff will wreck their creations (which, of course, is the right of the client) and that client staff doesn't really understand what wonders have been wrought (which is possibly true, but entirely irrelevant).

In short, if you cannot find a very good project-specific argument for staying with a project longer, reconsider your motives for wanting to stay. While it is possible that you would be able to convince your client of the need for more time, it should be harder to convince yourself that you should do so. Make yourself the toughest sell in this area of your work.

Responsibility to Clients

While your responsibility to your client is obviously involved as you consider the requirements of a client project, the notion of responsibility to your client encompasses a great deal more than the simple dictates of the project. You and he made an agreement. To the extent possible, you wrote it down. There are, however, in addition, the unspoken responsibilities that go with your roles as consultant, professional, and perhaps friend/advisor/colleague/associate. These responsibilities go along with the basic long-term kinds of consulting relationships. If, therefore, you have chosen a one-shot kind of consulting or a single-project focus for your practice, you can skip this section (and the next, as well).

Along with your roles as professional and expert goes the notion that you know more about your area of expertise than your client (and virtually everybody else) ever will. Your job has been to teach him and his staff some things about parts of what you know. This means that, even at project end, you will know a great deal more than he and will see pitfalls and potential problems of which he can have no idea. Under these circumstances, what is your responsibility to him and his company?

To some degree, it is a matter of personal belief. There is no right answer. If you structure your practice so that you generally work in fields and geographic areas in which you have unlimited potential clients, it probably does not matter from a professional/business perspective what view you take. If your fields are limited, or if your former clients are likely to talk with your potential clients, however, how you treat end-of-project responsibilities may matter professionally. It does matter to your clients.

And *that*, for me, is the critical factor. I want clients to be satisfied over the long term. And the only way to achieve that is to consider, as part of my responsibility in any project, seeing to it that the client's long-term objectives for the project are met (or explaining in very clear terms why they cannot be met). A fairly stark example might illustrate the issues.

I recall one client who wanted me to develop the initial projections for a start-up company. The purpose was to prepare figures for a key investor in the proposed company. This investor, though an old acquaintance of my client, was in an essentially different kind of business and had little understanding of the business my client proposed. His interests and those of my client would inherently diverge when the issues of ownership and the disposition of earnings arose. My client was a neophyte in business (then). I could see the coming divergence. He could not.

The agreement we made was that I should develop the initial projections and work with the investor's accountants to reach conclusions about the viability of the project and about the investment potential of the deal. As the process began working, I saw that my client needed information and support far beyond the simple development of a set of figures. He needed to become aware of the effects of different ownership schemes and of different distributions of the proceeds of the company. He needed, in short, a rapid education in how businesses work and are financed. To provide it would go well beyond our basic agreement. To fail to provide it would leave my client open to forces he could not yet see (although I could).

In essence, I assumed the agreement he would have made had he been able to see what I saw. I explained what I was doing and why as we went along. His underlying objective was to get the company going—but still to own a chunk of it once it was running. The initial projections were just a means to that end. I viewed my responsibility as a professional as assisting a client in reaching his end, rather than as producing a specific piece of paper.

As this project was about to end, a major reorganization in the proposed company was suggested. The investor's accountants offered to handle the reorganization of the projections. What was my responsibility then?

As I saw it, the rapid education of my client could not possibly make him competent to evaluate the nuances and appropriateness *for him* of the reorganized figures. Also, I believed it to be in his best interest to retain control of his numbers. I suggested that I do the restructuring. He agreed. In fact, I wound up doing more business with this client than either of us had expected. That was nice. But, more important, this client cannot look back on our professional relationship and conclude that I could have helped him make a better deal but that I chose not to do so.

While that knowledge is extremely important to me, it need not be so to you. Do be aware, however, that your clients *know* you know more than they in your field. That's why you're there. They expect, and I believe they have a right to expect, that you will use your expertise on their behalf. For most people, that includes performing tasks that your client *could* not know about but that you *should* know about as necessary to meet the goals the clients stated and you accepted. I have heard business owners who are still bitter about consultants who, years ago, failed to help in these ways. (They're almost impossible to sell. They are off consultants for life.) Briefly, I believe in working for the objective rather than to the letter of an LOU. It makes for repeat business, good word-of-mouth, referrals, and most important, good nights' sleep.

MAINTAINING THE RELATIONSHIP

As you might suspect, my view of my responsibilities to my clients extends beyond the formal end of the project. While yours need not go as far as mine, you should give some consideration to follow-up and to maintaining the relationships you have built. Repeat business is relatively easier to sell (assuming you did a good job on the first round), and since you already know the people, project start-up is easier. If for no reasons other than these, maintaining relationships is probably worth the effort and time it takes.

If your original sales approach was the long-term, relationship-building kind of process, maintaining your relationship with your former client is both easier and more difficult. It is easier in that you will still meet at all those meetings and groups that you met at prior to your work in the company. It is more difficult because you and your former client now have a different relationship. You have been close to him and to his business over a period of time. You have, thus, moved from colleague/acquaintance to something closer. You cannot backtrack, assuming that you wish to maintain a business relationship with this former client.

People in general, and your former client in particular, tend to assume that the most recent definition of a relationship will remain in place. In a situation in which you wish to change but not end the relationship, you therefore must serve as change agent. And you must do this without alienating your former client. This means that you need to forge a modified relationship to replace both friendly colleague and close confidante—perhaps something like close colleague or whatever terminology you prefer.

Keep in mind, as you consider this problem, that your former client has a stake in continuing to view you in the old pattern. With you as a close friend and personal advisor, he will feel safer as he moves his company into the new ground that you developed for it. If he spoke too freely to you while you were at his shop, he will feel safer with you under his eye and in the category of friend. Given this, if you move to detach abruptly or clumsily, he is likely to be both frightened and angry. He will, nevertheless, remain a member of all those business groups that comprise your market.

This pattern does not always develop. It is, however, frequent enough to warrant consideration. You can tell when it is developing if you pay attention. You can recall (from notes, if necessary) what this person's behavior was like at meetings prior to your project. With whom did she tend to talk? Did she circulate a great deal? Did she spend a great deal of time with you? And now? Has the pattern changed? How has it changed? If for example, your former client used to circulate, talking with at least half the people in a given room, but now sits rather quietly by your side, you have a problem. And you need to deal with it quickly, if for no other reason than the fact that *you* need talking time at those meetings to develop business.

Perhaps the easiest way to begin to detach an overly clinging client is to enlarge the group. If Ed is becoming a problem, make sure that you walk into the meeting with George. Ed is welcome to join you both, of course. That makes three of you, rather than a closed group of two. You have effectively prevented the kinds of discussions you do not wish to have because Ed is unlikely to begin them with a third party present. Equally important, if there is a third person, you will not feel constrained to remain attached during the whole meeting. You can leave the group to take care of your other business without leaving poor Ed sitting all by himself. Ed is unlikely to feel angry (disappointed, perhaps, but not angry) because, after all, you did come in with Old George. Pretty soon, Ed is likely to resume his former meeting behavior, and you are painlessly off the hook.

One method of preventing the clinging-former-client problem is also the approach of choice for maintaining contact with former clients in general. The idea is to help your client to feel comfortable in what he is doing and secure in the knowledge that you will be there if really needed for help in the follow-on to your project. I find that two things are fairly effective in conveying those feelings (in addition, of course, to the education and training process that I generally consider part of the project). First, I make clear to my clients at project ends that they can call me if a project-related problem crops up. And I make sure they know how to reach me. Second, I check in periodically.

Letting people know that they can reach you, if necessary, has two effects. First, you send a clear message to the effect that you have no intention of disappearing into the night, never to be seen again. This is a common fear about consultants—that they will create some fantastically complicated construct and be long gone when it breaks down. (This is no idle fear, as a great many owners and executives will attest.) Assuming you really are prepared to support your work, telling your client so will allay some concern. Many clients will track you down at least once for no good reason, just to see whether it works. If it does work, the calls are likely to disappear. In general, however, just knowing that they *can* call you is reassuring and will prevent calls in most cases. (See earlier comments about client dependence, a situation in which this will clearly *not* work.)

In addition to client comfort, knowing that they will call at need is reassuring to you. No frantic phone calls equals no problems. You have a satisfied client. The only caveat here is that you consider taking these calls only about issues related fairly directly to the work you did. You do not want to encourage or support a general dependence on you by your client or his staff.

While telling your clients that they can and should call when necessary must occur before project end, I generally try to be the first to place a call related to the project. Since you helped develop it, you will know what is supposed to occur in whatever process is going on. You know the critical or particularly difficult points. How would your former client react to a call at one of those points just to find out how things are going, whether there is a problem, and/or how the schedule is working out? She'd probably be overjoyed—especially if she could report that everything was going just fine, thank you.

In an exchange like the one just described, you are accomplishing any number of things at once. First, you have given your former client an opportunity to crow. Second, if there *is* a difficulty, you can probably prevent it from becoming a full-blown problem. Third, you have demonstrated conclusively that, though you have gone, you have not forgotten them and have not abandoned their project. Fourth, assuming all is going well, you have provided yourself with a personal pat on the back for your own good work. Finally, you have provided yourself with an opportunity to find out what *else* is going on in that business or industry. This last may lead to further or related work for you.

Timing is everything in this callback process. You can probably time your first call to forestall client panic calls. Future calls should be placed at key points, but with decreasing frequency. The general idea is that as time passes and implementation or operations proceed, there is decreasing likelihood that you will be required on your old project and increased client confidence in their own abilities.

This does not mean that you cannot consider and discuss potential new projects. Calling back former clients invites those clients to discuss new or different potential projects with you. You have demonstrated that you can get the job done (on time and within budget?). You have demonstrated that you are not the great disappearing consultant. You have demonstrated that you are trustworthy, along with your other virtues. You are also good. What more does any client want? These qualities, and your client's experience of them, make you the instant frontrunner for further work in your field with this client. You simply need to give him the opportunity to tell you about what has to be done.

I provide former clients with the opportunity by calling in every six months or so—even long after a project is over. I have maintained the business acquaintanceship so that these calls are easy and enjoyable. They naturally revolve around our joint interests in relevant fields. Thus, even if I do not hear of an exciting new opportunity in this company, I may hear general industry news that I could not have picked up elsewhere. This information may give me the needed edge in doing something else for another potential client. The former client usually gets any small new tips that I have picked up or developed. These are generally things I could never sell but that are useful to her nonetheless. Everybody wins something. And everybody enjoys it.

Essentially, this kind of callback program is the bridge to the new relationship of close colleague. The basic trust has been developed, and a deeper relationship results. Because this is a slow building process, it is fairly easy to identify and isolate those clients who are looking for a free ride. These have been described earlier and need not be discussed again. Suffice it to say that after the calls directly related to ending your project with such clients, do not call again. You are unlikely to gain work, information, or enjoyment from further contact.

Part 3

GETTING DOWN TO *YOUR* BUSINESS

8

A PRACTICE IS NOT JUST A BUNCH OF PROJECTS

Using the techniques and approaches described in this book, virtually anybody with any experience at anything, who is also marginally intelligent and somewhat personable, can probably sell a consulting project. However, most people who have sold one or two or who are already convinced that they want to become full-time independent consultants *for a living* recognize that they really want more than simply to be able to perform random tasks for smaller-company clients. In short, they want what they are doing to make rational sense to them.

There is a nagging (and true) sense that, unless their work as a whole has some measure of coherence, they will not prosper (or have any fun) in the longer run. Two aspects come into play here. First, without a coherence to your work, you will have no focus, no way to determine what business you should chase or accept. This leads to the chicken-without-a-head syndrome, in which you attempt to do anything that looks as if it might produce money. Your efforts grow progressively more scattered. You develop neither expertise nor a solid reputation. Additional work becomes more difficult to sell. You feel frazzled and pressured most of the time. In short, you not only stop enjoying what you are doing but you also lose control of what you are doing and tend to make less money at it as well. Like the chicken, you eventually keel over.

Perhaps more to the point, your clients, smaller-company clients in particular, need to believe that you know what you are doing. If you cannot explain clearly and coherently what your own business is all about, they rapidly develop serious doubts about your ability to help them determine or modify what *their* businesses are all about. On the whole, this is not an unreasonable position. This is why chickens without heads eventually lose their clienteles.

There is a great deal to be said for the ability to discuss what you are doing in clear, concise terms. Stories abound about how the ability to define what you are doing really sells. My personal favorite is attributed to Louis Mayer (of MGM fame). He reportedly required each proposer of a new project to write the project definition on the back of one of his business cards. If a proposer couldn't manage that, no further hearing was given the idea. The clear message was that if a proposer did not understand his project clearly enough to convey its essence in a (very) few words, he would be unlikely to produce a clean, clear, concise product—and Mayer was certainly not going to fund the attempt.

While this story may be apocryphal, the underlying point is well taken. Inability to explain what you are doing probably *does* indicate lack of clarity about what you are doing. Fortunately, developing a good description of your practice field(s)—in essence, transforming a bunch of projects into a practice—is usually not difficult. The next section offers some approaches to beginning this definitional process.

DEVELOPING A COHERENT PRACTICE DEFINITION

There are three main approaches to developing a beginning practice definition for yourself (and your clients). They are identified rather irreverently in the following list and explained in the following subsections.

> The Topsy method,
> The Whatever-Turns-You-On method,
> The What-They-Really-Need method.

It should be stated at the outset that this initial definition need not remain your definition forever. As you operate, new wrinkles or even new fields may grab your interest. Your practice definition may, as a result, become more narrowly focused or it may expand to encompass newer, related areas or issues. The definition you develop now will serve you for now. It should not constrain you forever. Remembering that your current definition is alterable is extremely helpful in permitting you to begin the definitional process at all. It makes the whole process less scary.

Topsy

This method is so called because, like Topsy in *Uncle Tom's Cabin*, it "just growed." In this case, the "it" is your practice definition. It just grows from an analysis of what you have already done and a series of assessments of how well you liked doing each project and how well you performed in each instance. While this sounds as if you need to have been in business before you define your business, it is not true. You can use any kind of work-related projects for these assessments.

The underlying theory of this approach is that one gravitates toward doing what one enjoys and does well. You define what your practice is by defining what it has been in the past. You look at your personal trends as you consider defining them better and extending them into the future. The key to this process is total honesty, including honesty in the area of what you messed up and why. Remember, nobody will see it except you. And kidding yourself is a disaster in any endeavor.

First, make a list of all the projects you have done in the last few years or months (depending on the lengths of your projects). You should aim for a list of at least ten items so that you have enough material to consider in some depth.

Second, for each item on your list, write down what you particularly enjoyed and did not enjoy about doing each item of work. As you perform this task, try to exclude the effects of unique features— the particular group of people you were working with, for example— and focus on the generic qualities of the work. You liked the opportunity of working with a group, say, despite the fact that those particular people were a pain. At the same time, write down the generic factors that were particularly distasteful to you. You detested, for example, interacting with personnel representatives or spending so much time in the client's offices or whatever.

Third, consider the content and work mode of each project on your list. For each one, identify your role, e.g., expert, worker, team leader, etc. At the same time, pinpoint the topic(s) of the content of the project. Do this on two levels. First, list the nitty-gritty. Second, show the generic type of project content. An entry for one of my projects, for example, might note that I developed an interactive database system to help a client track project progress and professional time commitments. I would also note that this project was basically a "building managerial controls" project. Arrange your project lists so that generic types of project content ("managerial controls") are grouped together for further evaluation.

Fourth, working with the grouped lists, write down—being brutally frank if necessary—how well you did and how comfortable you felt performing each major part of each project. Do *not*, at this point, consider whether the client was pleased or displeased. I have found that frequently clients do not know enough to see when they are getting a substandard product (and all too many poor consultants are still operating and giving the rest of us a bad name because of this). The ability to please your clients can generally be seen as a separate skill, not necessarily related to the quality of your technical work.

Your final project sheets might look something like the following. Your columns can (should) be wider to accommodate more detailed comments and descriptions. This format is offered simply as a starter. There is nothing magical about it.

Finally, consider skills that cross all project lines, and make a separate list of them. The list might include the abilities to please a client, to sell a project concept, to write well, to communicate with all levels of employees. Again, being as honest as you can and remembering that you can burn the list when you're through with it, rate your abilities on these items.

When you have completed consideration and grouping of the projects you are analyzing, sit back and take a new look at the sheets. Start by addressing the issue of the fields in which you work well and enjoy. Remove from your list the types of projects you clearly detest. The first time I tried this, I found myself with virtually no list remaining. This was a clear signal that I needed to shift my practice signifi-

Project Analysis Sheet

Category: Staffing Working Committees					
Project	Skill	Role	Liked	Didn't	How Well Done?
(Client) Work rules	Researching precedent	Expert	Research; attention	Having to be evenhanded	Very (A+)
	Reporting	Reflecting opinions	Writing	Lack of decision-making role	Fair (B−)

cantly. I also had to resign myself to doing stuff I did not want to do while I built on the items that would move me into more congenial areas. One does need to eat. But at least I knew what I had to do and what I had to work with.

The next part of the analysis is to consider clear deficiencies and major strengths. This is done by looking at the roles you have played in your projects and at the tasks within projects in terms of how well you do them and how much you enjoy them. This analysis can help you pinpoint areas for personal development. Having identified a problem, you can take steps to remedy it. Or you can decide that you'd rather skip that field entirely. If, for example, you seem to enjoy working in a field in which computers are the coming wave but you felt uncomfortable relating to computers in past projects, you might take a course that will help you over the basic problems. (You needn't tell anyone. You can even go to some other city to take it.)

Essentially, your objective for the final part of the analysis is to build your ideal project mix. You need to pay attention to the fields in which you have enjoyed working (and in which you have done good work). It is the generic groupings that you devised, however, that will prove most important in clearly defining your practice. These will help you see any threads that run through your work and will help you discern patterns among your projects.

From my own experience, I know that there are often patterns that one fails to see because they are obscured by the details and by what others tell you about what you do. When I first started my practice, I really believed that I was running two virtually separate practices. I worked with health services costs/reimbursement and with smaller companies in start-ups and management control.

When I performed this kind of Topsy analysis, I discovered two major interconnections. First, most health services entities are classic smaller companies. Second, the underlying basis of all my project work was in developing monitoring and control systems for companies. I had been listening to the experts who kept telling me how different and unique the health services business was. I had been responding to those who saw my work as being in two vastly different fields, those who kept asking me how I could perform two such different kinds of work. I had begun to wonder myself. As my analysis showed, despite the fact that I hadn't seen it and certainly hadn't been able to describe it coherently, I had developed a coherent practice. The simple exercise described here will let you see such patterns, as I did, with fresh eyes.

Whether or not you choose to use this kind of analysis to sharpen your practice definition, you will find it useful to perform periodically. It not only forces you to evaluate what you are doing and how you are doing at it, but it also highlights significant selling points in your past work that may be useful in acquiring new work. In short, however valuable a Topsy analysis may be in defining your business, it is likely to become at least equally valuable as an ongoing marketing analysis technique for you.

Whatever Turns You On

This is the "sales" model of practice definition. While it sounds something like the Topsy analysis, it proceeds from an entirely different set of starting points. The Topsy method assumes that you know what you are doing, even if you can't explain what you are doing. This process assumes that you are going to be starting fresh. While the Topsy method defines a practice from past history, this procedure asks you to define what you want to do, independent of practically everything else. Therein lie both its strengths and its weaknesses.

Essentially, the method is to consider what you want to do (and, it is hoped, what you are competent to do) and to define your practice as composed of projects in the field(s) in which you wish to work. The underlying assumption is that expertise or experience in almost any field can be harnessed, put to work, and sold in any number of ways at various different levels. The trick in defining your practice is to target scopes and levels that make sense to and for you (and will make sense to your clients).

In a first pass, you might try visualizing your most desired work day. Then use what you saw to pinpoint the characteristics of the kind of consulting practice you wish to develop. If, for example, you saw yourself sitting in a client's boardroom making a presentation, you might look into strategy-level applications of whatever your expertise is. If you saw a group of rapt listeners gazing up at you on a podium, perhaps the applications you should consider lie in the field of training. An image of you in shirtsleeves on a shop floor reworking a machine has still other implications.

Your second pass should be based more on your skills, talents, and experience. Armed with information from your analyzed vision, list whatever you have that could be brought to bear on the situation in which you saw yourself. While you were making that board presentation, what were you talking about? What were you teaching that group? As you list your qualifications for the job you are defining, also consider what else you will need to have to pull this off. Consider, before you commit yourself, what you will have to do to make yourself a viable candidate for the job that your practice definition represents. Part of your analysis needs to be an assessment of what it would take for you to get those extra qualities.

Third comes the hard part. You have to choose from among all possible options those with which you will start out. The problem is that most of us in this business are intensely curious about large numbers of things. We also tend to be tinkerers. We get bored easily. The recognition that by making some choices we are excluding other choices makes the process one that appears fraught with danger for us. As you go through the process, it is helpful to remember that you are not excluding everything else for the rest of time. You are only, in fact, making an initial definition, excluding some things for the time being.

While working from an existing project base (the Topsy analysis) is frequently easier for us, this more free-form process permits us to examine our strengths and preferences with minimal reference to what we have done in the past. This facilitates consideration of the possible rather than the merely expedient. It also has particular value in some specific situations. If, for example, you are truly disgusted with the kinds of work you have been doing and intend to make major changes, this might be a good approach to use to consider what you might wish to change *to*. It will also help define the steps you will have to take to get from here to there.

There is some downside to using this method alone, however. In a project-based analysis, there is good reason for believing that someone will pay you to perform the services that come under your practice definition. Someone has done so in the past. It is not necessarily true that people will pay for the services you saw in your vision. Assuming that you are planning to be a consultant for a living, this is a rather critical issue.

It must be noted that using your preferences as the sole basis for your practice definition is dangerous. Definitions developed in this manner need to be tempered by a good market analysis and may well require some modification to enable you to eat regularly and put a roof over your head.

What Do They Really Need?

You know your field or fields. You have probably been working in and around them for years (even if you have not yet put together a clear definition of what your fields are). That gives you a reasonable basis for standing back and looking at what that field really needs and does not have. You can then build your practice (initially) around providing solutions to that (those?) problem. This is the marketing approach to selling: finding a need and filling it. It works in all fields.

Defining your practice using the marketing approach is a two-part process. You begin with a market analysis. This need not be a formal study like those they told you about in marketing class. It is more like a structured and systematic consideration of major issues or problem areas in your field of expertise. It helps to have listened to other participants in the market as they griped about what they would really like but could not find anywhere.

With this kind of background in what is missing or difficult, you begin to consider what you could bring to the problem. If, for example, you have worked in a number of industries, consider whether a solution that exists in one industry might be applicable, if modified, to a different industry that is currently having difficulty in a similar area. Alternatively, your familiarity with a number of industries or fields might lead you to put the pieces of the problem or issue together differently. This different perspective might suggest solutions to industry problems that people without your particular set of experiences might not recognize. In short, consider what unique vision you can bring to this industry or field.

Using a marketing-type approach to practice definition assumes that you understand each industry and field well enough to determine accurately what is and is not applicable across fields. As you perform this practice-definition process, then, note those areas in which you need to do some work to determine or ensure that you are not constructing your practice definition on a bed of quicksand.

In addition to these potential cross-fertilization issues, a marketing approach to practice definition may require another set of analyses and some live testing as well. A potential difficulty for many of us is that we may be too far out ahead of our markets. They don't yet know that they need what you are offering. To pursue a practice definition based on filling that market need would involve you in a lengthy, expensive, and "iffy" process of education before you could hope to sell anything. Unless you are independently wealthy, this approach palls rather rapidly.

I found this out the hard way. In fact, I was so loath to believe it that it took me two very expensive and frustrating lessons. The first one came in the early 1970s. It occurred to me that hospitals were basically just businesses that sold services. As such, it probably would be nice for them to know what it cost them to do business and to maintain some basic controls over their operations. I got the verbal equivalent of rotten tomatoes from most administrators in the field. Hospitals were *not* just businesses. They did *not* sell services. They provided health care. I could not possibly understand their business if I did not understand that.

Well, history proved me right (this time). I think wryly of the competitive advantages I could have built for client hospitals had they listened and worked with me back then. Some of them are now struggling to build those same systems in a cost-constrained, highly competitive situation. I, by now, am bored with the issue.

But did I learn? Of course not. In the late 1970s, it occurred to me that certain kinds of smaller companies had the kinds of cash flows that would permit them to take advantage of rising interest rates coupled with the increasingly competitive market in the banking industry. I developed a simple cash management system that would facilitate having their money make money. Nobody was interested.

Now, of course, everybody does some kind of cash management. You undoubtedly do too.

Finally, I got the message. The trick is to be only slightly ahead of your market. You sell something at that level and then work with them as you initiate them into your vision for farther down the road. Not only does that get your clients to where you believe they should be but you get to eat in the interim.

Unfortunately, the only way to determine if you have a concept that is too far ahead of its time is to test. I suggest that you test fly the concept as you propose other related things. Watch the reactions carefully and gear your responses and emphases to them. If you are going with a marketing definition, remember that the market is the key.

Any combination of these methods that works for you will serve the basic purpose—reaching a coherent practice concept that you can use to describe what your business is really about. In fact, as in most cases in this business, anything that works is OK. The critical point is to use *some* method to arrive at a definition of what you will and will not (or can and cannot) do that will offer you a focus for seeking and performing consulting work.

You will find uses for such a practice definition in a number of instances—even if you don't want Louis Mayer to fund your company. You will want to use it in letters, proposals, and if you choose to develop one, your brochure. You will use it as a handy way to tell potential clients at meetings what you do (and may be able to do for them). For the first time since you started this business, your friends and relations will be able to tell *their* friends and relations what you do. Most important, however, your practice definition will serve as your own central reference point. It will become the basis for your objective-setting processes and your evaluation routines.

SETTING OBJECTIVES

Once you have decided where you want to go, the next step is to determine how to get there. This is one of the primary operational uses of your practice definition. The idea is to determine the steps and performance levels on those steps that will result in the coherent practice you envision.

This is not an easy process to undertake, but it is really helpful in the longer run. It is difficult because it forces you to consider what is possible and what is likely and to commit to performing at some desired level. All these administrative-type things probably contributed to your desire to leave whatever job you left to start this company. The differences—and they are significant—are that now you get to define and determine the objectives and that nobody else ever needs to see either your objectives or your performance appraisals. In your own operation, they exist solely to make your life easier.

Now that sounds as if I am contradicting myself. I said that objective setting makes your life harder and easier. Both are true. It is harder at the beginning, when it seems much easier just to drift, picking up consulting projects as they present themselves or as you see a random opportunity to sell something. It makes your life easier at any time after the initial objective-setting sessions since your goals and objectives define what business you want to chase and the market(s) in which you want to chase it. It may help to think of the written document you are about to produce as a modified autopilot. Once you have done the initial programming, your route is set. (You still have to work at meeting your plan, though. Unfortunately, nobody has yet come up with·a foolproof way of convincing consulting projects to define themselves and walk in your door.)

As a general rule, consultants (and would-be consultants) should set goals and develop objectives in two main areas. The first, overall business building, is discussed here. The second, billings, clients, collections, etc., forms the basis for your management control system. As such, the process of determining those goals is discussed here; more is found about how to use them in Chapter 9.

Let me add a personal tale here. For the first years of my consulting company, I was one of those who did no planning or goal setting. I *knew* where I was going and what I was doing. Besides (I discovered upon later reflection) I found the notion of having to perform up to my own ambitious and exacting standards very frightening. In addition to the difficulties this approach caused in terms of trying to tell people what my business was all about (discussed earlier), I had virtually no control over the business of my business. While I could and did control project quality and progress, I could exercise no control over what projects came my way. I could not really sell (having little coherent notion of what I was to sell or to whom to sell it). Because I could not target my efforts, they remained scattered and, consequently, much weaker than they could have been. I could not really build a business, although I could and did add more work. In short, I had no idea of what I was doing or any handle on how well I was doing anything in my business life. I felt out of control all the time and at the mercy of pure chance. This is a truly rotten feeling—particularly for those of us who need to project a cool, competent, in-control image for our clients.

Eventually, I found my position so distressing that I was driven to a more formal approach to goal setting. I discovered that it wasn't so bad after all. I still have difficulty committing to specific performance goals, but then, I suppose, I always will. I keep telling myself that nobody knows but me and that the entire thing is a competitive game I play with myself. That approach works for me. It lets me do what I need to do in the objective-setting area. Use whatever works for you. But do *some*thing that helps you track what and how you're doing. When I think of the years of random (wasted) effort that could have been spent really building my practice. . .

Business Development

For business development purposes, you will need to consider objectives in a number of areas:

Practice segments,
Market segments,
General business development efforts.

Sit down with the practice definition you developed in the last section and really look at it. How are you going to get from where you are to where you said you wanted to be? You will do it by breaking down the requirements into manageable tasks and then performing those tasks—just as you do with the projects you do for others. (In this process, consultants, as a group, tend to be very like the shoemaker's children. While we do good project analysis for others, we tend not to do it for ourselves. It does help to try to detach from the fact that this is your practice. Try treating the process as if you were developing a business plan for a client.)

Consider your practice definition in terms of the kinds of business you intend to do. If you have targeted two related fields or areas you want to develop, consider each separately. Suppose, for example, your practice definition is built on providing assistance in marketing analysis and product suitability. You would structure each as a separate line of business. Then you would decide, based on your preferences tempered by your assessments of the sales potential of each kind of business, the proportional mix between the two.

The next step is critical: the assessment of who is likely to buy what you will be selling. Depending on how you approached your practice definition, you may have already given some thought to this issue. Now is the time to make those thoughts concrete. A good method of defining your primary target segments is to consider the characteristics of companies that might benefit from the service you will offer. Then consider the characteristics you cited in terms of the industries in which they are frequently found. Your prime targets are companies with those characteristics in those industries.

An example might help here. Suppose you plan to sell time management services. You know that those who might benefit are professionals who bill time to various clients or projects. You also know that tailoring and installing your system will cost at least $30,000. You are planning on selling your system on the basis of recovering time that simply falls through the cracks. Thus, you need firms with *many* professionals if you are going to be able to make your case. You would calculate *how* many based on your estimate of lost time per professional or some such figure.

Your list of potential industries that fit your required characteristic list would include, at least, law firms, accounting firms, consulting companies, and perhaps various kinds of repair and construction groups. With this list and your minimum size cutoff, you can proceed to target companies that are good prospects for your practice.

Now, for each industry segment you identified as having good potential, law firms, for example, how many do you think you should be able to sell during the next planning period? Define what your planning period is, and voilà!, you have an objective. Walk through this procedure for each market segment and each practice segment you identified.

As you work through this process, keep firmly fixed in mind your staff and time limitations. You may be the only person who will be out there developing business. If that is the case, you will also, I hope, be performing project work as you do so. Consider how much time you will really be able to devote to building or reorienting your practice and still keep paying your bills. Also remember, however, lest you be tempted to give your development effort short shrift, that if you are not developing business now, later you may find yourself with no current project work through which to pay those bills.

Most larger consulting companies have methods of tracking the potentially useful contacts of all their employees. Many of them require their professional staff members to target the number of new contacts and renewal contacts they expect to make in a year—even though they may not result in any business at all that year. The theory is that repeated contact creates the same kind of atmosphere of mutual trust that I discussed earlier as part of the selling process.

I raise the issue again, here, because expanding your field of contacts and maintaining existing contacts is a time-consuming process. Since we all tend to be overburdened with work and specific development, general business development efforts are frequently de-emphasized. We are too tired to go to that meeting. We cannot make time to work on that committee. But because so much of smaller-company consulting work develops through these informal channels, giving in to that inertia can be suicidal in the longer run. If you structure such activities into your specific objectives, you will find yourself making the time for them that you know you should. Therefore, put them in.

Bases for Operational and Financial Controls

You may have noticed that the objectives described in the last section dealt only with how many clients, calls, contacts, etc. you would achieve. You probably also noticed that, by themselves, meeting goals stated in that way would not necessarily make you enough money for corned beef hash, let alone caviar and champagne on the Concorde to Paris. It would be possible for you to exceed all your development objectives and still be a financial flop. The objectives discussed in this section are designed to ensure that if that is going to occur, you will at least know it in advance. (Cold comfort perhaps, but it beats total surprise.)

Your second set of objectives (tied closely to your business development objectives, of course) is designed to fill that gap between performing projects and doing business. In this step, you determine what you need to make and how you intend to come up with the money. Done properly, this step will also provide the baseline for your internal monitoring and control systems. (These are discussed in greater depth in the next chapter.)

Consultants who want to work with smaller-company clients appear to fall into two groups, based on their feelings about money. There are those who have no trouble defining their operations as businesses, designed to (among other things) make money. (Please note that this need not be their *sole* aim, or even their primary one, but they view it as a legitimate objective with a high priority.) The second group seems to find the entire issue of money somewhat demeaning. They tend to avoid the issue whenever possible and to take money almost reluctantly from clients for legitimate, frequently excellent, work.

This second group is a dangerous group to be in. These consultants tend to undervalue their services. Clients, taking their cues from the expert, thus view their services as less valuable. Interestingly enough, the result is not more business (because of lower price tags) but less business (resulting from service that is perceived as less valuable). If you would naturally fall into category two, then, start really thinking about what you are telling your potential clients through that attitude. Consider making changes.

With that out of the way, we can proceed to how to figure out a reasonable set of financial and operational objectives for your practice. Your first move should be to determine how much money you need or want to make from your consulting practice. Here, you are limited somewhat by your choice of smaller companies as clients. While a Big Eight consulting group can sell half-million-dollar projects to clients, that kind of sum may well represent half of the year's gross receipts for some of your clients. Of course, you are unlikely to need platoons of staffy types to service your clients, so your expenses are likely to be lower than theirs. If you are really looking for champagne and caviar, however, you may have chosen the wrong business segment in which to consult.

Whatever your personal attitude, your business and non-business lives demand certain levels of funding. One way that you might start determining your needs is to use your most recent salary as a base. Remember that you now have certain expenses that your employer used to cover—part of your Social Security tax, for example, and probably your health insurance costs. Your business may make additional requirements in and of itself as well. For example, you may need to join clubs and business groups. You may need to travel and entertain potential clients. The point here is that rather than aiming simply to replace your net income, consider the ways in which your requirements will change as you change your status.

Once you have a total requirements number, you need to split it up among your practice and market segment objectives. When you are through, each objective should have an estimate of financial gain or cost attached. This also, of course, requires that you consider the lengths of time and amount of work involved in the kinds of projects you expect to sell in each field. The net of the figures should come out to your total requirement for the period. The underlying notion is that you should be OK if you meet your objectives. If you exceed your objectives, you have that much extra.

Because, particularly in the early rounds of objective setting, you tend to overestimate what you can do, it is generally wise to structure your pricing to meet all your requirements at something less than 100 percent of your objectives. This gives you a cushion in case of overambitious plans. But, perhaps more important in the long run, it forces you to test out a pricing structure above what you probably think is realistic. As you find that people will buy at the outrageous rate, you may decide to make the new pricing level permanent. More information about developing consulting rates is provided in Appendix B.

In all cases, the key to effective objective setting is the terms in which you state your objectives. You have told this to clients often enough, no doubt, but a reminder here cannot hurt. Your objectives in all these areas need to be specific; that is, you must state, preferably in numbers, *exactly* what you are committing to produce. This might be "three new clients for marketing analyses" or "fifty-two contacts with potential new clients" or "twenty-nine initial sales calls." The "what" matters less than the specificity of the statement. It gives you the clear goal for which to shoot.

In addition to the commitment to the number, you have to include in your objectives statements and in your commitments a time element. State clearly *by when* you will have signed those three new clients, for example. This raises the issue of planning periods. Here, just be realistic. You are unlikely to be able to see what is going on in some areas in under a quarter. For most consultants, actual project sales fall into this category. In other areas, sales calls, for example, the period can be a great deal shorter because you are more directly in control of the activity. Set your time frames based on the flows you expect in your field, tempered by your reactions to deadlines and target dates. Never forget that you are building this entire construct to help yourself do your business better.

Beyond the what and the when, you have options. If you are likely to quibble with yourself over "what counts" in a given category, for example, you might want to decide in advance what counts. If you will probably agonize over priorities among your objectives and/or tasks, consider adding predetermined priorities to your written goal statements. Essentially, the idea is to take care of the items that will be troublesome *to you* at one time, periodically and thoroughly. Thereafter, you will be able to take care of business without worrying about those details and within guidelines you determined for yourself. Your system can be as complex or as simple as you need to fulfill those basic functions.

SELLING BENEFITS

This chapter talks a great deal about what you will be selling in your consulting practice. You have not been reminded since Chapter 3, however, about two key features of what you are selling. Nor have you been reminded of what people are buying while you are selling. This final section constitutes those reminders. They are singularly appropriate as closers to a chapter in which you define what you want to and think you can sell.

Throughout this chapter, you have been asked to consider what you want to sell. Only occasionally have I raised the rather basic issue of what clients want to buy. There are really only two things to remember about what clients buy when they buy your services.

First, consulting services—even productlike services—are intangibles. The client cannot generally touch directly the result of your work for him. He knows that in advance. You need to become supersensitive to that fact. What he is really buying is you. His confidence in you is what lets him lay his money (and, perhaps, his company) on the line behind your advice. No matter what else you may be selling, given the intangible nature of your product, you are really selling you.

Second, clients do not buy the features of what you are selling. They do not care that your chiropractic service can be provided on their work sites. They may well not care that your service is less expensive than Doctor Dan's down the street. What a client will buy is perceived or expected *benefits* to her or to her company. She will buy the notion that using your service can cut down her absenteeism from lower back problems by X days per year and reduce her workers' compensation claims by as much as Y dollars a year.

Given the fact that clients buy benefits, whenever you sell whatever you decided to sell, be sure to think your offering through from the client's perspective. After every proposed sales statement, ask yourself, "So?" When you finally get to the part of this discussion with yourself where you smile and say, "Aha!", you have probably reached a salable benefit for your potential client. That is where you should start your sales routine.

9

THE BUSINESS OF CONSULTING

You now have sold a project or two and defined your practice in a way that makes sense to you. The only task you have left is to ensure that your practice gets you wherever you wanted it to take you. That task is only partly concerned with the content of your consulting practice. The rest is organization and control.

This chapter addresses the organization and control areas of your business life. It specifically focuses on three major segments, each of which often becomes an issue for an independent consultant at some point in business development. First, it addresses issues related to billing and getting paid. Second, it discusses the use of resources— computers and personnel. Third, it discusses ways of figuring out how well (or poorly) you are doing at your practice and of figuring out what to do about it.

MONEY MATTERS

Remember when your parents and/or your teachers reminded you that if you were good at what you did, you would be recognized and rewarded? Well, I wouldn't want to believe that they actually lied to us, but it *is* clear to me that they were misinformed (or the world has changed significantly since they last looked or they weren't talking about independent consultants to smaller companies or all of the above). Getting your reward is often difficult.

As far as I can figure it, the underlying problem is that people like to hang on to their money. Those who are clearly willing to pay you frequently cannot do so because *they* are small and other people and companies want to hang on to *their* money. The net effect of this situation is that you spend a great deal of time and energy worrying about how to pay your bills, keep a roof over your head, and put food on the table. This is a waste of your time and energy. And you do not *have* to do it, if you set up your business properly from the beginning.

Setting up properly is comprised of three segments: setting rates, billing (and maintaining backup records), and collecting. Each topic has been touched on in earlier chapters. This section brings the information together, reiterates frequently ignored items, and expands on critical issues. It also discusses some related difficulties that independent consultants often report and proposes ways to deal with each difficulty.

Setting Rates

For a consultant to smaller companies, setting rates is a balancing act. Alternative disasters are setting them so high that you price yourself out of the smaller-company market and pricing so low that you render your service worthless in the estimation of your potential clients. Striking a middle ground can be done by paying attention to how the large consulting companies price (above your upper end limit) and your educated instinct about what will appear too low. Your pricing structure also needs to take into account the amounts of money you will need (want) to maintain your life and practice as you wish them to be.

Independent consultants tend to one overriding difficulty in the rate-setting process. They frequently price their services too low. Some simply underprice their time. Some undervalue their probable contribution to their clients. Some merely believe that prices should really be based on what it costs you to produce the services. This error often includes serious flaws in the ways costs are analyzed. The net effect of this difficulty is to leave you always scrambling and always worrying. I know. I spent years doing it.

Consider the process and what you are really offering to sell. First, you are selling one severely limited item—your time. Your time is limited by reality. You have only X hours a day, Y days a week, etc., just like everybody else in the world. This part of your product/ service is entirely nonrenewable. If you waste an hour or fail to sell an hour, there is absolutely no way to recapture it. You cannot replenish your stock.

You are also selling something unique: your particular set of skills, knowledge, experience, and expertise. These are what make your time worth buying. It adds the market factor into your pricing calculation.

Essentially, when you set your rate(s), you need to be able to cover all your costs and expenses and any profit you want to make by selling the number of hours and days of your time and effort that you realistically think you can sell. This defines your rate-setting process for you. First, you add up all your costs, expenses, and desired profit. Then you estimate the amount of time you will actually work for paying clients. You divide the former by the latter to determine working rate. You then consider where it falls in your range of acceptable rates and pick a number you like. For example:

General personal expenses	$ 40,000
Profit desired	20,000
Business expenses	40,000
Total expenses	100,000
Number of days you expect to be able to bill	125 (about 50 percent of total)
Per diem rate	800

As you go through this process, remember to count all your costs. You will have to pay for them whether you remember to count them into your per diem rate or not. Also remember that, while you will probably work more than 100 percent of working time (250 days per year) on your business, the only thing that counts is the time you can bill a client for. Those days (or hours) have to be priced to cover your needs. Also speaking from experience, I can tell you that there is nothing as demoralizing as working ninety-hour weeks only to discover that you are still worried about how to pay your bills.

This process sounds simple—and it is—once you get used to the underlying idea that your time and expertise really are seriously valuable. It has helped me enormously to consider my proposed rate or price for a project in relation to what my work is going to save the client or do for the client. You can, in fact, develop prices on this value-based billing basis. In cases where you can quantify the expected savings or benefits to your client, you might want to take some percentage of those savings and spread that amount over the number of days you expect the work to require.

Expected savings (benefit) to client	$1,000,000
Your share @ 10 percent	100,000
Number of days of professional effort required	100
Per diem rate	1,000

Voilà! a new per diem rate. If your value-based per diem consistently exceeds the rate you calculate by a cost-based method, you might reconsider your basic pricing method or your profit targets (or your lifestyle).

Keep firmly in mind as you tackle this part of your practice that studies show that you, like most independent practitioners, are likely to underprice your work. This occurs both in terms of the value offered relative to more expensive providers and in absolute terms. We seem to have collective difficulty in asking the market to pay what we are worth—despite the fact that most of us can prove our value in dollars and cents to prospective clients and to ourselves.

Undervaluing is a difficult habit and mindset to get out of. It helps to keep value-based examples of your work in your mind—or on a paper pinned to your refrigerator, if necessary. One project that I frequently use in this connection was billed to my client at $85,000. While this sounds astronomical (or did to me at the time), my work showed the client how to save $4 million in the first year and as much as $5 million a year thereafter. As rates of return go, the client undeniably got a fantastic deal. I should have charged them more—but by then, of course, it was too late.

Billing and Record Keeping

Once you've set the rate and cut the deal, you have a real, live client to whom you have to send bills to get your money. You may call them invoices in your line of work, but the bottom line is the same. You have to ask the client for money directly. This is another frequent stumbling block for independent consultants.

There seem to be two major problems. First is the attitudinal problem discussed previously. Many independent consultants seem to have difficulty asking for money—particularly big money. The second is a tendency to underestimate the amounts of time spent in performing work for a client. I do not mean here such always knotty, but valid, issues as whether you charge and how you charge for travel time or waiting time or telephone time; rather, the problem lies in thinking about whether the client has really used the time or whether it *should* have taken so long. The first problem I cannot help with, other than to alert you to the facts that it often exists, that it is a real problem, and that you are not alone. There are techniques for dealing with the second problem.

My favorite story in this regard comes from my brief stint as a staff auditor for a Big Eight accounting firm. Having not yet learned how to do the work properly, I thoroughly messed up a report. The senior auditor on the job caught the problem and showed me the error of my ways. I, of course, said that I would take the stuff home and fix it on my own time. After all, I figured, the client was certainly not responsible for my inexperience.

The senior flatly vetoed that idea. He pointed out that there would always be someone as green as I on that audit. While the next guy might not make the same error, he probably would do something equally dumb and equally time consuming. If they estimated the cost of the job based solely on good time and the good intentions of my offer, next year (and in subsequent years) they would estimate too low. The firm would then be forced either to eat the loss or run over budget. Their estimates, he said, had to reflect how long it really took to get the work done, warts and all. I learned.

The moral of this story is that, while your client is not responsible for your mess-ups, all jobs have them to one degree or another. The issue is whether you consistently eat the cost or share it explicitly with your clients. Each of us has to come up with an approach about which we can feel comfortable. In real life, the client will never know. But before you eat the cost as a matter of routine, consider that such items are really part of your costs of doing business. Thus, they are, at least in part, payable by this client. They will be paid either through time charges (numbers of days) or embedded in the per diem rate. Recognizing them specifically through time charges permits you to track them and examine them. They may not even be entirely your fault.

Another favorite trick of consultants when developing their bills is to underestimate how much real time was spent on a particular project. This is easy to do since we frequently spend time in numerous small pieces rather than in large chunks. Thinking time, for example, generally comes in spurts. Worse yet, it doesn't *look* as if you are doing anything at all. Many consultants feel shy about charging this time. Without that thinking time, however, what are you really offering the client? Reduced to its ultimate, that thinking time is usually exactly what he's paying for. Track it and charge it. The time it takes to administer a project is similar, as are project-related false starts and all the time you take dealing with your client.

Lest you believe that this is small change we are talking about, let me tell you about a law office client I had. They had the sense that a great deal of unbilled time was being spent with clients on the phone—ten minutes here, fifteen there. They sure were right! We built them a simple phone-time tracking and monitoring system and found thousands of additional dollars a month in billings. These were all legitimate charges to clients for time spent with them or on their behalfs on the phones. We also found that some clients recognized the lack of billing for phone time and had been taking them for serious rides.

The point here is that, if you track all time, you have the option of billing or not billing for it. If you don't track it, you will never know how long it really takes you to get a project done. You are quite likely to find that clients make disproportionate use of such small item time. If unbilled, it all gets folded into your rates. All your clients then share equally in the cost. This strikes me as more unfair than billing specifically, but it's your choice.

Once you decide to find out about how much time you spend in small chunk time, you will have useful information for future estimates. For this purpose, you will probably want to track client, activity, and amount of time. Your system can be as simple as careful notes in your calendar or as sophisticated as a computer database system, but the tiny amount of time you spend logging billable time will pay off handsomely in the end.

Because it provides better records for both you and your client, and because it makes your client feel more secure, I recommend including in your bills more information than is absolutely necessary. Mine tend to describe briefly the tasks addressed during the professional time being billed for. They also frequently include a brief project status report. The extra information shows clearly that you have client communications at the center of your practice—even at billing time.

In addition to how much to bill, independent consultants often have difficulty with when and how frequently to bill. My problem is actually sending out bills. What works best for me—not foolproof, but not bad—is to consider a bill as part of my promise to the client, one of the deliverables in our agreement. Thus, I try to box myself in by stating in my LOU, that "It is our practice to bill on a monthly basis for professional time expended and out-of-pocket expenses incurred."

Sending client bills is a good thing to be prompt about. From your own perspective, slower billing means slower payment, which in turn means that you may have to pay your suppliers and creditors more slowly. Also, oddly enough, slow billing worries clients. The reason may be some concern for their product, if their consultant cannot even get bills out on time. Slowness may well also mess up their budgets. Perhaps more to the point, the larger bills for lengthier time periods may give clients pause. In short, see whether you cannot perform this part of your job better than I do. Bill when you promised your client you would. Both parties to the deal will be happier.

Collecting

Sending bills, however, doesn't help unless you also ensure collection. This topic has been discussed in some detail in Chapter 4 under the heading, "Billing and Collections." My practice is to send a second invoice with my next bill (which *does* get out on time) and to talk with the client about the status of my payment. As noted earlier, how long I will carry a client depends on his previous payment history with me and what I already know about him, his business, and its difficulties and cash flows. I have been known to arrange delayed payment schemes and/or time payments based on the needs of a particular client business. My purpose is to assist the guy's business, not break it.

As you are already painfully aware, no doubt, one of the hazards of working with smaller companies is their erratic payment histories. Temporary cash flow difficulties may put your payments on hold more frequently than they might in larger companies. To some degree, your payment priority is determined solely by the owner. Thus, you may be subject to some capriciousness. Also, when the owner of a smaller company is distressed, the most frequent response is not to discuss matters but to not pay.

All these factors argue for developing and maintaining close and continuing contact with your owner/client. You want, for example, to find out that she is distressed before the project is done and has decided not to pay you. You may need to establish your priority on a personal basis. It is rougher not to pay a friend.

Should these approaches fail, you are looking at a nonrecoverable loss of time. If you think a collection agent might be the answer in such situations, know that they take up to 33 percent of what they collect. They are also unlikely to be interested in the size and frequency of business they can do with you. There is also the political issue of whether you stand to lose more than you could gain by using this collection approach. Given its costs and potential effects, consider carefully before you go this route.

Clearly, the best approach to dealing with collections is not to let the situation get out of hand in the first place. I almost never deliver product until at least a sizable portion of the fees have been paid (and the checks cleared). In this particular area, I firmly opt for letting the client take the risk. I *know* I'll deliver the product. It's the payment I'm not sure about.

RESOURCES

A second area that often causes concern to independent consultants is the appropriate use of resources. While this, of course, is a matter that depends more on specific practice content and individual taste than billing and collections, there are some general tendencies and approaches that seem widespread and, therefore, worth noting. The discussion has been divided into two parts—equipment and personnel.

Clearly, to some extent these two resources are connected. In time-honored fashion, people can substitute for capital and vice versa. Ultimately, the choices are yours. A brief outline of what hard equipment can do and of alternatives to standard staffing patterns, however, might be helpful as you define and develop your business.

Equipment

A given independent consultant tends either to love gear and gadgets—hard assets—or to avoid them. A good, profitable consulting practice can be developed either way (assuming that, if you want it, you can raise the initial funds to purchase the stuff and you reflect its cost in your pricing scheme). The issues here are whether you *need* all that stuff and what it can do for you if you have it. The image issues of office furniture and location have been discussed (Chapter 4), so this section focuses on computers, phone systems, and similar items.

Essentially, each of us gets to decide our work mode through decisions about what equipment we will use. If we choose to work really alone, we are committing to some significant investment in the equipment that will let us do the required jobs ourselves. If we choose to have staff to do various jobs, gear will not be so critical. In this trade-off, a microcomputer generally becomes the key item of equipment. It certainly has for me.

The attraction of a computer lies in its flexibility. I cannot tell you what it can do to assist you with the work you do for clients. You know its potential in that area. What I can do is talk a bit about the ways a computer can help you to manage and operate your business. I need to warn you in advance, however: I am a believer.

I came to be a believer from a standing start. I had managed to reach adulthood and acquire a business degree without ever having laid a glove on a computer of any description. My introduction to microcomputers was very slow and tentative. In fact, I owned one for more than a week before I gathered the courage to turn it on. Shortly thereafter, however, I was hooked.

What got to me first was its word processing capability. What my computer printed out looked better than any material that had gone out of my office ever. Since I wrote drafts anyway, using the computer with a word processing program actually reduced my writing time and made production time virtually nonexistent. I could produce more in less time. And I didn't need to hire a secretary to achieve all this. The thing made me look great. And looking great is a subtle sell.

I have since learned to use my word processing program for mailing list operations. In my particular business, this can include sending personalized letters along with copies of new articles to my client list and potential client list. It includes occasional small group mailings. It lets me differentiate what I send by category of client easily and without redoing everything numerous times.

My word processing program also does yeoman duty in helping me manage form letters and such variants as LOUs. Essentially, you can store these items and recreate copies or copies of parts of them at will. Standard letters and forms no longer even take any thinking time.

I went to school back when spelling counted for everything. They also taught you how to do it. If, however, you are one of those folks who never quite got it or who grew up in later, more permissive, times, current word processing programs now generally include spelling checkers and hyphenation functions. The program will tell you when you have misspelled or mistyped and offer you alternatives. Since your reader(s) may be among those of us who care about such things as spelling, ensuring that yours is correct may be a useful function. It certainly cannot hurt. You need to be aware, however, that computers do not read for context. They will only let you know when your error is not a valid word. Nothing is foolproof.

After word processing, I discovered the joys of spreadsheets. A spreadsheet program essentially duplicates the green gridded accounting paper that used to be so intimidating to nonaccountants. Because they encourage you to think about your business numbers in terms of underlying relationships and to express business relationships in formulas, spreadsheet programs actually help you to understand your business. In addition, they encourage you to test what occurs if you alter or modify relationships or factors. In short, they let you fool around easily with changes you might want to make. They offer a risk-free chance to see what would happen if. . .

Specifically, spreadsheet programs are extremely useful for keeping track of your accounting data and tracking your cash flows. They offer a simple way of considering your internal business relationships, for example, how much you get back for every dollar you've invested or how much you make for every dollar of billings. They also let you play with projections for your business and estimates for particular projects. You could see what would happen, for example, if you raised your billing rate by X dollars or what you could lose by going three days over estimate on a fixed price contract. In short, they take the sheer drudgery out of pushing your own business numbers. Once you have built the formats, you're home virtually free.

I am still in the process of learning the wonders of databases for my business on my microcomputer. Essentially, a good database program helps you to maintain files that you can then relate to one another in different ways and from which you can draw data for reports. The key here is the ability to pull together data from various sources. They also let you store large amounts of changing information efficiently, making changes and additions easy.

Databases are particularly useful for such files as call lists and client lists. Using them, you can keep track of who you called when and the results of each call. You can then sort through to find key characteristics of your successes and, if necessary, common traits among your failures. You can track project progress and performance against estimates. You can track the efficiency and effectiveness of your staff members or project team members, if any. Again, once you have built the systems, getting at the information you need in the format you want is a snap. You will hear more about potential uses of your computer in the next main section of this chapter. It deals with keeping track of what you're doing.

As is clear from this discussion, a computer is hardly a necessity for operating a successful consulting business. It can be of significant assistance, however. I would be lost without mine since I have discovered that it increases my output and decreases my time and cost. It also simplifies my record keeping and filing. It is not absolutely necessary, however.

Beginning with a computer requires a sizable investment in time and money—nothing to take lightly for those of us who sell our time. You need to have a fairly clear idea of what you want to do with it before you make your purchases. You need to determine the software programs you will start with, the compatibility and interchangeability of information among them, and the hardware you will use to run them. You probably should also consider compatibility with your clients, expandability of your systems, and availability of support in the market for your choices. As you can see, that is a great deal to decide.

After you bring the creature through your door, you will have to invest the time to learn how to use at least the basic functions of your programs. You will build the basic formats for your spreadsheets and design the basic databases for your initial projects. Plan to spend significant amounts of time cursing and screaming at your computer, your spouse, your kids, and anyone else within range. But once you have the basics aced, it will all have been worth it. You will never stop learning additional wrinkles or neater ways of doing things, but you will have gotten your computer to do the basic levels of the work that you brought it in to do.

As a side benefit, I have found that people almost automatically believe something with numbers if printed out by a computer: While, of course, the output of the computer is only as good as what went in, the believability factor is sometimes of value to you in your dealings with others. Thus, you might choose to offer printout from a spreadsheet program, for example, instead of columns of typed information. For reasons unknown, it will be believed more readily.

Whether or not to purchase equipment other than computers is usually easier to decide. The technological content is lower so we each feel competent to assess the alternatives well. We know the purposes of the gear better and can see the trade-off service costs more clearly. Thus, deciding to buy a copier rather than going down to the local copy shop becomes an economic decision, tempered somewhat by personal preference. Deciding to buy an answering machine trades off the equipment cost against the cost of using the services of people. In this one, some assessment of the reaction of client callers to each might be the tempering factor.

The key notion is that, if the function really is necessary, it has to get done somehow. Equipment acquisitions (with their attendant front-end costs and potential tax and ownership benefits) can substitute for service cost (with their recurring charges and general unpredictability, but also with their human touches). The choices are yours. Just remember that they are only largely, not entirely, financial.

Personnel

Personnel cost is frequently traded off against equipment cost. This trade-off, however, works best in support functions—typing, copying, etc. The issue discussed in this section is a great deal broader and less cost oriented. The issue here is how to get your project work done most efficiently and effectively. Each of us cannot do everything equally well all the time, and we cannot do it all at the same time. Given this situation, how do you arrange it so that your projects are signed at acceptable prices and that they get done well?

The obvious answer is to buy outside talent. The next question concerns the best ways of doing that. There are three parts to considering your options. First, you must address the issue of what you really need. Second, you need to figure the costs of each of your alternative approaches to meeting your need. Third, you need to consider the noncost advantages and disadvantages of each of your alternatives. After this consideration, you can choose an approach for a particular situation. Your best choice may not be the same in all cases.

What you really need should be defined as a set of skills, talents, or capacities. Do you need a database specialist? Or someone to enter data into a database? You also need to consider how often or for how long you expect to require these skills.

What it will cost to provide what you need depends, of course, on how you choose to cover your requirements. If you choose to hire someone full time, it is likely to be less expensive than using a skilled person virtually full time, but on an outside service basis. If you need the skill only infrequently, it will be less expensive to buy on a service basis.

The noncost factors you need to consider include your need to feel "ownership" of staff working on your projects, your expectation of how your clients will react to "nonowned" personnel, and how much you can (or need to) trust the people you are bringing in as outsiders.

You have essentially three main kinds of options among which to choose. First, you could try to do it all yourself. This invites not only disaster but also ulcers and incredible fatigue. You cannot be fantastic at everything. You are unlikely to love doing everything. You have only so many hours in a day. Most important, some things cannot be learned on the fly—no matter how brilliant you are. And I am not among those who believe that it is called a "practice" because that's what you do on your clients.

In specialty fields, in particular, be extremely wary of the do-it-yourself approach. Offering legal advice, for example, can get you in lots of legal trouble (unless you have the appropriate certification). Accounting and data processing can also be problems. In fact, in a specific situation, attempting almost any specialty cold can produce serious side-effects and harm to your operation. In short, if a company needs the equivalent of neurosurgery, do not whip out your *Brain Surgery Made Simple* and read as you cut. Get the guy a brain surgeon. You'll sleep better at night. More to the point, you may have time to sleep.

Your second general option involves hiring the talent directly into your company. You can do this on either a part-time or a full-time basis. Your part-time/full-time choice should be dictated by the length of time or the frequency with which you expect to need that particular skill and by the market for that skill in your area. If there is great demand for few practitioners, you are unlikely to be able to use half-measures. The skill owner will be in the driver's seat. Also, you might not want that same person working for other consultants in town. Your marketing plans may dictate the need for an exclusive on that service.

Adding staff on a full-time basis is often trickier than it looks. If you need a really skilled person, it may be very expensive for you to purchase. You may find yourself looking at a partnership arrangement or no deal. Under the best of circumstances, you have suddenly acquired a significant ongoing cost that you need to generate the work to cover. This will skew your work toward projects using this new, expensive skill. It is possible that, over time, your practice will depend as much, if not more, on this new skill (person) than on your skills. Thus do practices get away from their founders.

If the person you add is not so expensive as to bend your practice, you may find yourself making money from the efforts of another for the first time in your life. The larger consulting practices develop billing structures that take one-third of the per diem as the practitioner's salary, one-third as contribution to company overhead, and one-third to profit for the firm. While you will incur increased overhead in personnel, support, and administrative costs, this formula frequently results in big profit—if you all can generate the business to cover it. Hiring thus lets you leverage the work of others into profit for yourself (or for all of you, if you're so inclined).

The third option is the one I have chosen to date. It creates a loose group of independent professionals of various specialties. Members of this group work together on projects as necessary and independently when it makes better sense to do so. This approach has two major disadvantages. First, clients have trouble understanding that you are for real even if you do not have three thousand hot-and-cold running staff people. Second, to make this work, you have to be able to place a great deal of faith in the integrity and honesty of those with whom you choose to work, not to mention their skill. My general assumption is that each of us will pursue his or her own interest and will not be particularly up for taking over the work of the others. In general, each of us is far too busy to poach. It is, however, difficult to get such a group together.

The advantages, to my mind, far outweigh the drawbacks. First and foremost, I do not have to support a payroll. This leaves me freer to take on jobs or to pass them if it makes better sense to do so. Second, I can choose the best possible set of skills for a specific client project. I do not have to worry about some guy, unused and costing me money, back at the office. Third, I can work with a self-directed group. Its members know what they need to do. Management becomes coordination rather than supervision and control. Work thus proceeds more smoothly and with a minimum of fuss. Finally, though I may not make as much in overrides (their rates tend to be appropriately high), I can still give the client a better financial deal than can a supplier who is supporting a large staff. In my view, everybody wins. And it is up to me, through my marketing messages and my reputation, to convince potential clients that this is true.

My beliefs notwithstanding, the choice is entirely yours. How you handle these basic staffing issues can be one of your most important strengths. If done badly or thoughtlessly, it can sink your operations. Word of poor work and/or inappropriate staffing travels fast— particularly within the smaller-company community of a relatively independent region.

KEEPING TRACK

Whatever choices you make in the process of defining and developing your practice, it is absolutely critical that you keep track of what you are doing, how well you are doing it, and how your strategies are working. While nobody has the right to expect never to make a mistake, at least we should make new ones rather than repeating the same old ones. It helps if we learn from both errors and triumphs. Your tracking system should be designed to help you to do that.

It is amazing how many of us put off finding out how we are

doing. We seem to think that, when we left the corporate world behind, we left all kinds of measurement and control behind as well. Actually, all we did was rescind our implied permission to others to define our measurements and controls for us. Now, we're on our own.

There may also be an element of fear in the general avoidance of controls and monitoring. Perhaps more than most people, consultants need to believe that they are in control of situations and can make them work out right. As long as they do not look closely at what is really going on, they may be able to sustain any illusion. If they actually look, they may find that they are not in control at all. This could be a devastating discovery. Hence, they don't look (and maybe it will work out in the end).

Of course, if they are not in control and they do not look, there is no way they are ever going to gain control. What these folks set themselves up for is an ever-increasing level of anxiety. It feeds off not knowing what is going on in their businesses, not understanding what makes them work, not knowing how to turn them around and gain control. In beginning the task of finding out what is really occurring, the hardest part for these people is taking the first step—deciding that, yes, they will look at the reality.

The best time to design your tracking system is at the same time as you develop your practice definition. The redefinition process lets you begin fresh. However, if you have put off finding out how you are doing, you can start at any time.

Your monitoring and control system is defined by the set of questions you want to answer. These will probably include:

1. How are you doing relative to your objectives?
2. How are you doing financially?
3. How well are you meeting project estimates of time and cost?

While your list may be longer or shorter, try to consider only the broader questions at this stage. Your first step is really defining what you want to know as a basis for further evaluation and decision making.

The second step may be the hardest part of this process after the decision to monitor your progress. You figure out what measures make sense given the questions you are trying to answer. Many give up along about here, claiming that there is no reasonable way to measure something as intangible as a consulting service. If you join that group, you risk never knowing whether you have succeeded. If you eventually feel successful, you are unlikely to understand why or how this occurred. Consequently, your successful feeling will also feel precarious, accidental. It will have happened to you rather than being something you made to happen (back to the control issue again).

Assuming that you decide to tackle this task head-on, the best place to start is with the quantified practice objectives you defined earlier (see Chapter 8). There, you stated what you would view as success in a number of practice areas. Having these statements reduces your current question to how you might measure progress toward those goals. Once you determine appropriate terms of measurement, all you have to do is define reasonable interim steps between where you are and where your objective would place you.

A simple example would deal with a financial issue. Dollars is clearly one of the easier standards of measurement. Everyone understands it (more or less). Suppose that your practice objective was to achieve sales of $500,000 by Practice Year 5. Your practice currently bills $100,000 a year. You might set interim goals as follows:

Year 2	$150,000
Year 3	300,000
Year 4	350,000
Year 5	500,000

To determine how you're doing at meeting this practice objective, you need to track only how much your company bills. Billings thus becomes a key item of information that you collect, track, and analyze as a matter of routine:

Objective → Measurement definition → Tracking of measure

When you get your quarterly (or annual) billings information, compare it with where you determined you should be if you are going to reach your goals. If you are running behind, you want to try to pinpoint why. You also might want to consider whether your goal was too ambitious in light of the emerging reality. If so, you might revise the goal. If not (and be honest, now; there's nobody there but you), then you need to figure out how to get back on track. If you are running ahead, you might consider why you are ahead. If it looks as if you underestimated your potential, you might revise your goals upward. If you just did a great job, try to isolate where and how you did it—and how you can duplicate the feat next quarter (year):

New data → Comparison with goal → Analysis of differences → Action

But you have no doubt noticed by now that the single piece of information, dollars in billings, is really a composite of a number of other things. It is the result of the number of projects you perform, the billing rates at which you perform them, and the number of staff you have working on them, among other things. Each of these also has components that you might want to consider in real life, but we're keeping it simple here. If you really want to begin to control your main success measure, you might want to break it into some component parts and track each part separately. Then you could see what was helping you to meet your objective and what was hindering.

Your original $500,000 objective might translate into:

	Current	Year 5
Number of projects	2	5
Average billing rate	$800	$1,000
Staff	1	3

Your new "Items to Track" list would then include:

Clients	Rates/hours billed
Staff members	Staff time billed
Projects	Size of project

Given what you already know about the consulting business, you might also want to add to this growing list of items to track:

Number of contacts (because X contacts result in one call)
Number of calls (because Y calls result in one project sale)

As you go through the practice objectives you set for yourself, you will begin to develop a long list of what you need to capture information about. Before this gets out of hand, let me remind you that your monitoring and control system is supposed to help you take over your practice. It should not be permitted to take over your life. Hence, once you have developed your full list, you will want to start weeding. Your objective is a manageable system that tells you what you really need to know about what is going on and where you are without swamping you in data once a month. This can be achieved by categorizing your data needs and choosing your key indicators with care.

The broadest categories of information needs that I tend to use are financial and operational. To some degree, your accountant and Uncle Sam define your financial requirements. See how you can use the data they require to serve your own needs as well. You will be collecting it anyway. Some key items in the financial category include the measure in our original example, Billings, and:

Salaries	Accounts payable
Accounts receivable	Profit
	etc.

Operational measures are generally one step in back of the financial results numbers; that is, these measures combine or reorient one or two pieces of basic financial information. They may consider detail behind a single financial item. They are inherently analytic rather than simply descriptive. Such measures might include:

Billable professional hours	Support versus professional dollars
Performance against budget	Time performance against
etc.	estimates

When you get all your lists together, go through them to determine which would be relatively easy to capture as they are generated. This explicitly recognizes that the purpose of your monitoring and control system is to support your operation rather than reorient it. Consider also which pieces of information are so important to your analyses that it is worth an expenditure of some effort to get them. Design a paper flow that lets you capture them and a format that will let you store and display them easily. This is one area in which a computer and a good database and/or spreadsheet excel.

At the same time as you design the data capture procedures, also design the reports and analyses in which you will use each piece of data. The timing of this part of the process ensures that you will not forget why a piece of information seemed so important when you decided to track it. It also serves as a crosscheck on whether you really need the item. If you are not going to use it (have not incorporated it directly or indirectly in some analysis), why focus on it in this system?

When you have completed this step, you will have a full-scale management control system tailored specifically to your operation. If you just let it sit there forever, looking professional, you will have wasted your time and energy. As you build it, you should also determine how and when you will use it.

Because our business tends to be so frenetic, our own planning and analysis are often catch-as-catch-can. While expedient, it leaves you almost as exposed as if you had done no preparation and consideration at all. The only answer I have found to this problem is the same one I have come to on the issue of vacations: Make the time, and make it inviolate.

In the case of using your monitoring and control system, this means ensuring that the items you have decided to track are entered *as they occur*. It means that you schedule a specified amount and period of time on at least a monthly basis. This time is devoted solely to considering what is going on in your own business. Your monthly planning session should provide you enough time to review the data collected; compare it with your estimates, projections, and objectives; highlight and assess the significance of any deviations; and decide what, if anything, you need to do about all this.

If your office is a continuing circus, plan and review somewhere else. Once a quarter and at least once a year, plan for extra-long, extra-intense sessions. Should a special problem arise (or threaten), add extra sessions to your cycle. Even if all appears well, do not skip your session. Appearances can be deceiving. Follow the established process, determine that everything really *is* rosy, and give yourself an explicit pat on the back for carrying it off so well. You will have earned it.

By the time you complete this building-up/whittling-down/
cycle-development process, you should have a very clear sense of
how your particular practice will function. You will have pinpointed
its critical indicators. You will know what moves them up or down.
You will have highlighted those things that you can do to affect them.
You will have planned time for analysis and decision making. In short,
you will already have come a great distance toward exercising control
of your own business realities.

And, after all, wasn't that level of control one of the things you
were after when you set up your own operation?

10

STRATEGIC ISSUES: HOW AND WHAT YOU WIN

The sum total of the major choices you make regarding your consulting practice embodies your strategic approach. Assuming that you thought carefully about those choices as you made them (or, at least, as you read through this book), they will exhibit a pattern. When you identify the wellsprings of this pattern, you will have identified your strategic principles. Once you identify them, you can use them directly in your decision-making processes.

As you will see, your strategy is the most fixed reality of your current business. It defines what business you will do. It assists you in determining the specific work you will take on. It influences your marketing approach, staffing methods, and payment terms. While your strategy is certainly alterable, serious alterations generally require wholesale rethinking of how you do business. Changes in objectives and methods must follow changes in strategy or vice versa.

It is helpful, therefore, to consider how to identify strategic patterns and the implications of different strategies for consultants to smaller companies. Alternatively, you could define a strategy first and then follow its implications in building your practice. That relationship between strategy and practice is the major focus of this chapter. The chapter goes even farther, however, discussing things that help and harm consultants to smaller companies as they pursue their strategies. It ends with a brief discussion of what you win when you win at consulting to smaller companies.

WHAT ARE WE DOING HERE?

Suppose that when you started consulting to smaller companies you had a good one-shot idea that you wanted to sell. You developed, say, a neat spreadsheet approach to handling banking/cash management functions. You would provide the templates and the needed software. Since all that was required, at that point, was plugging numbers, you would also run a client's initial-period data. Your main objective at the time was to make money and break away from your former employer.

You could consider your strategy and approach to your work as follows:

Type of practice: Product type
Marketing: Letters, cold calls, demos
Follow-on needed: Little to none
Pricing: Fixed, based on savings of your method
Key requirement: Volume

As you proceeded to sell hundreds of your templates/programs, you began to get distressed about being on the road all the time. You grew concerned about always selling, never getting a chance to be thoughtful or build a relationship with anyone. In short, you were getting bored and anxious. You didn't want to give up riding your cash cow, but you did want something more. You decide to hire a salesperson to maintain your templates business while you shift your focus toward helping companies to manage their banking relationships better, a spin-off from your product-type business.

Assuming you could pull off this major shift, let's see what would happen to your business profile. Since you are keeping your product-type business, you would have a line of business that still looks like the preceding one, but now you would need a staff to run it. That changes your cost characteristics since that part of your business now has both to support its staff costs and produce enough extra to make it worthwhile for you to bother with. Your part of the strategy change, however, will produce a whole new business.

Type of practice: Individual efforts, expertise
Marketing: Development
Follow-on needed: Medium to high
Pricing: Based on professional time spent
Key requirement: Reputation and track record

While you could expand the descriptions and refine the con-
trasts, these items are adequate to demonstrate that the change in
what you want to do constitutes a change in the way you will have to
do it. You will have put yourself in a whole new ball game. This is a
fact that many consultants, particularly those in as undefined a field as
smaller-company consulting, tend to forget to their detriments.

Some of the big guys fail to notice this too. I have especially
enjoyed watching some of the Big Eight consulting groups in health
services try to cope with changes in the industry. The bulk of their
businesses used to be in preparing Certificate of Need applications.
These were the projections required by state governments before
they would approve expansions for hospital facilities. Despite their
protestations to the contrary, it was basically product-type consulting—fill in the blanks.

In recent years, the mad dash to add capacity has slowed in the
hospital business. Regulatory emphasis has shifted to operating costs
and data. The big consulting groups have not really adjusted to the
shift. They have kept the same staffs. They have tried to maintain the
productlike nature of their service, substituting information services
and off-the-shelf costing systems for the old Certificate of Need forms.
Their size and commitment to products make it difficult for them to
respond quickly. Thus, they risk losing market share to more nimble
adversaries (who are now growing rapidly and being acquired by
larger companies).

Our ability to respond rapidly and appropriately to changing
conditions is one of the advantages of being small and independent. It
only works, however, if you monitor the markets in your industry or
specialty and if you understand how some changes in your business
will require you to make other changes. Re-examining your strategic
profile periodically can thus be viewed as an investment in continued
survival. Strategic shifts and their attendant changes take time to
accomplish well. If change sneaks up on you, necessary shifting time
will not be available. You will have given up a significant competitive
advantage.

WHATEVER YOUR CHOICES . . .

Being a consultant to smaller companies has some basic requirements, independent of the specific strategic choices you have made.
Such rules of thumb reinforce and support whatever strategy you
have chosen. They come in two varieties: the don'ts and the dos.
Each is discussed briefly here. They will need tailoring to your specific set of choices, but you don't need me for that.

Don't

This section is largely about keeping your promises to clients. If
you maintain a clear awareness of the implied and explicit promises
you make, you will not have to think about what not to do. The only
don't will be not breaking those promises. If, however, you are not
naturally tuned in to the agreements that underlie your agreements, a
brief review of two implied promises might be helpful. They are
highlighted because they are so critical to your client relationship.
Even though they are unlikely ever to be subjects of discussion
between you and your client, the two issues highlighted here create
subtle undercurrents that can enhance or harm your client interac-
tions.

The two biggest don'ts have been touched on before in this
book. They are noted again here because of their importance in
developing a successful smaller-company practice. The first has to do
with client perceptions of value. The second has to do with the kinds
of work you should not perform.

Consider going into a bazaar and bargaining for some item. The
seller lays out a price that you know is too high. You then offer
something you know is too low. When you finally come to an agreement, you take the thing home and spend a great deal of time and
energy wondering whether you could have gotten a better deal or
how well Jack did with this same merchant. You stop focusing on the
item you bought in favor of a focus on what you paid for it. When you
are the seller, this is absolutely the last focus you want your clients to
have. Yet you set up the same dynamic when you negotiate price.
Don't.

If you think about your last proposals written or estimates
developed, you will recall that you developed the project price estimate based on the estimated time and the price per unit of time. You
probably built your project in blocks based on the natural breakdowns

of tasks. If you do not want to adjust your price per unit of time (the price you place on your value) and you cannot reduce the estimate of time (because you gave the client your best estimate in the first place), what's left to play with? Answer: Project scope—the number and scale of the project blocks. These can be altered to reduce costs to the client. And that is all that should be changed in cost-cutting efforts.

Recognizing and understanding constraints on your client is part of your job. The larger part is recognizing and recommending what she really needs to achieve whatever you are working on. When these needs conflict, which is frequent in smaller companies, your client needs to know what the lack of money is costing her. Essentially, your willingness to reduce the scope of work, phase it differently, or use her people more extensively conveys two messages, both of which you want to send. First, it says that you will not haggle. The value you place on your time is not open to question. Second, it reinforces the notion that you offer value for money and that the only way to reduce cost is to remove some of the value.

If you have difficulty thinking of this in purely financial terms, think of it as a variant on delivering on your promises. The unit price for your time is, in a way, a promise—that is your fixed rate, the value you add. Your estimate of time required is a clear promise. If those key statements on your part are endlessly flexible, what can your client believe? *Don't negotiate rates.*

In a classically circular statement, the other major thing you shouldn't do is do things you shouldn't do. This refers to earlier discussions about understanding and respecting the extent of and limits to your expertise. It, too, reduces to an issue of not breaking your promises, although this has to do with an implied promise.

Essentially, when you hold yourself out as a consultant to a smaller company, you are offering to add expertise in an area in which the company lacks expertise. The implied promise is that you know what needs to be done and will see that it gets done. If you overreach your skills and expertise, you are not really seeing that it gets done right.

The client gets a bad deal for two reasons. First, when you work in an unfamiliar area, it usually takes longer to get anything done. The client is paying for your time (at expert rates). Second, there is no check on the value of the work accomplished. In your areas of expertise, you constitute a valid check on the work. Out of your sphere, neither you nor your client can really evaluate the work.

Despite the fact that you get the billings, you get a bad deal also. You may feel that your work is somewhat shaky. This is a rotten feeling. Even if you manage not to notice this, there is always the possibility that your work will not stand the test of time or of what the client needs to do with it. This can do serious damage to your reputation and, thus, to your longer-term business prospects. Finally, you do not get to build working relationships with experts in fields related to your own. Thus, you neither get to learn from them nor are likely to get referral or coordinating work from them. In short, doing work that is beyond your qualifications is a bad deal all around. Respect your expertise and keep pushing its edges wider, but *do not try to perform work that is not your work.* Refer it.

Do

The dos are also old stuff, but they bear repeating because they are really critical to your success. The key item that underlies all the others is to pay inordinate amounts of attention to your reputation. It precedes you with your clients. It can reinforce or undermine you before you even walk through your prospect's door. Once you acquire a bad rep, it is extremely difficult to erase, modify, or work around. Interestingly enough, as you have no doubt noticed, a good reputation tends to be only as good as your last project (or maybe two last projects). This disparity is why constant attention is required to maintain your sterling reputation.

Two stories may be of interest in this regard. I recall one consultant who had developed a reputation while in industry for having really creative approaches to problems and for being capable of inspiring employees to implement them successfully. He left industry to open his own consulting operation. He let his rep go to his head. He rapidly became known as a man who would ride roughshod over any opposition, including client preferences. As his projects began to pit client employees against client management, he stopped getting results. Pretty soon, he was forced to seek work outside his home-base state. His reputation spread ahead of him to neighboring states. Peace-loving and harmony-seeking potential clients wouldn't even talk to him, which is too bad, because he really did develop highly innovative programs and do good work. When I last checked that industry in his geographic area, I could not find this man (or his company) anywhere. Doing good work is not always enough.

A second consultant had been known, when employed in his industry, for his meticulous attention to detail. That guy could work numbers so that they would turn handsprings on command, a very useful talent. Unfortunately, the first few clients he could corral when he took his consulting operation on the road were fully prepared to use his talents in legal, but ethically questionable, ways. He came through with flying colors, preparing the necessary supporting documents and making convincing cases for his clients' positions.

His focus on the work itself, however, was his downfall. Other companies in his industry looked not only at the specific output of his efforts but also at the content of the positions he was supporting for his clients. They concluded that those positions were "sleazy," to use their term. The consultant was rapidly tagged with that epithet. Soon, he was getting work only from clients who wanted to "sleaze through" some position or other. In just a few months, he had gone from being a respected practitioner in his field to being a rather shady character to be avoided by those with integrity. There was no way he could recover. He left the region and got a job with a larger firm where he could avoid contact for a while. He intends to set up another independent practice sometime, but he will take a great deal more care about the purposes he supports next time around.

Either of the former consultants in these stories could have foreseen the effects of their actions on their reputations had they bothered to look. At early points in their independent consulting careers, they could have made the changes required to permit them to succeed or even to have facilitated success. Each ignored the underlying imperative of positive reputation building: *Pay attention to how others view you and your work.* This may be what floats or sinks your ship.

Two other key dos are also reflected in these two stories. First, *be patient.* Second, *remember who your client is.* Patience, though a virtue, is often difficult for consultants to smaller companies. There are two problems. First, developing the kind of business you need takes time, but most of us have the kinds of pressing financial requirements that are not always deferrable. As you have seen, however, taking the wrong kind of business can be fatal to your business and/or your personal dreams.

Second, we are, perhaps by nature, impatient types of people, particularly where our pet subjects are concerned. (That's probably a key reason why we are no longer in corporations.) We often expect everyone else to catch on quickly to what we are saying, to take their cues from us, and to move almost immediately to implement what we recommend. After all, we're the experts and that's what they're paying for, right?

Unfortunately, the world does not work that way. We get to recommend. Only the client can implement. Patience, often *infinite* patience, is required to *convince* the client that we are right. Smaller company clients can be very slow (by our standard) at deciding, especially when the decision is going to cost money. And if we push too hard or too fast, we can lose him entirely. We need patience to work with clients through to *their* decision points.

This leads us to the next overriding do—remembering who the client is. It is very easy for each of us to play to the gallery. This includes making ourselves look good in the eyes of client staff. We also like to strut a bit before our own staffs (if we have them). Occasionally, we have been known to misuse client information to enhance our images with other or potential clients. All this frequently backfires, as it did in the case of consultant number one, above. And when we lose focus on our primary job—assisting our client (person) to look good and do well—we also invite damage to reputation. We can so easily become known for being difficult to work with.

Sometimes, we do these things with the very best intentions. We believe, for example, that our recommended course of action is so important to the client's company that we are justified in using anything to push the client into implementation. Alternatively, we may go overboard in creating a countervailing force within client staff for our position against the delays of the client. The net effect is the same. The client loses control to us, and generally she doesn't like it one bit. Even if she does not throw us out immediately, the odds on implementing our elegant procedures lessen, and animosity builds. In short, she digs in her heels and, however good your original recommendations were, you're through.

At base, remembering who your client is is a simple exercise in consideration. As noted earlier, think about how you would feel if your positions were reversed. Evaluate your courses of action from the client's point of view. As I have mentioned frequently, really listening to your clients is critical to developing this ability figuratively to trade places. Remember that, while you will leave, your client will be there for the duration. Make personal concern and consideration a hallmark of your consulting practice. Interestingly enough, I have found that a reputation for this gets around almost as fast as one for the negative things.

These key dos and don'ts will stand you in good stead no matter what specific strategy options you choose. They are neither startling nor difficult. They can, however, give you an edge or two in winning the game you have chosen to play. And in a game as crowded and competitive as ours, an edge or two is more than anybody has a right to ask.

WHAT YOU WIN WHEN YOU WIN

You have made one strategic choice that I know I can applaud. You have chosen, at least tentatively, to work with smaller companies. It's not an easy choice, but if you win, Brother! do you win. While I am clearly biased, I believe that winning at consulting to smaller companies is one of the real highs available legally. And they even pay us for it.

I will reiterate some of the drawbacks, just so you don't think I have only rose-colored lenses. First, people cast questioning looks in your direction if you run your operation without staff and a fancy office. There is the presumption that you are really not serious unless you emulate the bigger companies. While this should not bother you in the least, it is rather disconcerting until you get used to it. This bias abates somewhat after you have been in operation for a number of years, but it never quite disappears entirely. As long as your clients and potential clients can be convinced that you are for real, the rest of the world doesn't matter much.

Second, in smaller-company consulting there is increased risk of not getting paid. This is because of the propensity of smaller companies—even those you assist—to go under. There is, as discussed earlier, also the higher risk that an owner will simply not pay you. There are techniques for minimizing this risk, but it is a greater risk in a small company than in a larger one.

Third, there is the increased hassle level that frequently comes with smaller-company work. As discussed in previous chapters, you will be dealing more directly in personalities than you would if you worked only in larger companies. While larger-company managers certainly have personalities, your owner/clients are used to having their own ways to a degree that managers are not. Moreover, virtually everyone in a large corporation has some control on his activities. In a smaller company, you are likely to be dealing with the last control. He *is* the game, and you have to be prepared to deal with that.

Finally, because your projects are likely to be smaller than the average large-company consulting project, it will take more of them to make your first million dollars. This implies a great deal more marketing time and effort. Still more time investment is required because of the marketing approach to which smaller companies respond. In fact, as a consultant to smaller companies, you are less likely to become a millionaire than if you develop a successful, well-staffed consulting company for larger companies. This is because the way you make serious money in this business is to leverage off the work of employees. To maintain control of a smaller-company practice, however, you will probably hire only a few employees. Hence, you should temper your expectations of anchoring your own 70 foot yacht off your own Mediterranean island.

Despite these difficulties and the significant downside risks (or, perhaps, because of them) the advantages of choosing this as your field can tip the balance toward a career of smaller-company consulting. First, you can work virtually alone or with a very small staff. While one of the first questions that a large-company manager will ask you is about the size of your staff, smaller-company people generally ask about staff only insofar as it relates to what they want you to do. Larger companies seem to measure your sincerity and commitment by the amounts of resources you throw at your business. The smaller ones understand, intimately, resource constraints and the notion that you do not have to be big to be good. That, for me, is a much more congenial (not to mention possible) position.

Second, you have a huge field of prospects in which you will not have any large-scale competition. Because of their cost structures, it is unprofitable for most large consulting companies to court and service smaller companies. The companies cannot pay the billing rates, and they don't generate enough business to make it worthwhile. Thus, below large-firm size cutoffs, you will not have to compete with the kinds of resources that the "biggies" could mobilize, if they chose. You will not have to spend your resources making competitive four-color slide presentations to accompany your proposals or bring in staff from the four corners of the country to mount a competitive, pre-award dog-and-pony-show. You can use resources where they are needed, and you can win the business competing against smaller providers like yourself. This seems to me to be a much more honest, appropriately focused kind of competition—in which one minds losing less (because there is a content-based reason) and loves winning more (because there is a content-based reason).

Third, you have a virtually endless market—unless you have a particularly narrow specialty. While there *are* only 500 Fortune 500 companies, the government and Dun & Bradstreet cannot even keep track of all the smaller companies. You will probably limit your market in specific ways—geographic, size, number of employees, etc.—based on your business needs, but you are extremely unlikely to run out of potential market in a smaller-company environment.

Fourth, since smaller companies tend to develop longer-term relationships with their advisors, unless your choice was for a one-shot, product-type consulting practice, one sell goes a longer way in this business. Thus, while your initial marketing job takes longer, it may well be compensated for by your repeated work for the same company (or for related companies that *your client* sells for you).

Fifth, it is *never* boring. Smaller-company clients always manage to find or develop a wrinkle you have never seen before or come up with a new set of constraints or requirements. This happens undoubtedly because they are small enough to have to work around obstacles as you have. Since everyone's solution tends to be unique, you will always be looking at a slightly different, always modifying, ongoing business.

The personalities you will meet in smaller companies also keep life interesting. Your clients will be generally strong people—head-strong, too—with some vision that is keeping them going. While they may be single-minded and have other flaws (just like all the rest of us), they are rarely boring people.

If you, like me, have a very low boredom threshold, this lack of boredom is extremely important in keeping yourself mentally fit and interested in your work. I have found that once I get bored with what I am doing, I stop doing it really well. I also stop wanting to to it. Both can be deadly if you own and operate your own consulting company. Both are unlikely as you develop a thriving, varied smaller-company consulting practice.

This part of my list could be very lengthy, but perhaps the most important factor in my continued choice of smaller companies lies in their potential for growth. As a consultant to a smaller company, you get to share in this continuing growth, to be a real and useful factor in fostering that growth. You can watch and help owners and their employees learn and apply new knowledge and understanding to the business. You get all the joys that supposedly go with teaching, *and* you get to watch and assist while change occurs rather than merely hoping that some day your work will bear fruit.

The purpose of this book is to assist you in dealing with the mechanics and the politics inherent in smaller-company consulting. I wish you well in your development, and I hope I have helped to create a strong competitor. Good honest competition is never boring and it keeps us all at our best. Good luck!

APPENDIX A

PARTIAL LISTING OF CONSULTING HOW-TO BOOKS

Listing in this appendix constitutes neither an endorsement nor a recommendation of a particular book. This book is not intended to be a complete course in basic consulting but a guide to better small-company practice for those who already have some notion about how to do consulting. The books listed here say they start from ground zero and include issues that this one does not—for example, how to write a proposal, how to get on lists for requests for proposals, how to do presentations, etc. As can be seen from the lengths of many of these books, treatment of any specific topic may well be brief and general, so I recommend careful scrutiny of contents before you decide that any book should be your main guide.

BERMONT, HERBERT INGRAM, *The Complete Consultant: A Roadmap to Success* (Washington, D.C.: Consultant's Library, 1982),125 pp.

COHEN, WILLIAM A., *How to Make It Big As a Consultant* (New York: American Management Association, 1985), 208 pp.

GREINER, LARRY E., and ROBERT O. METZGER, *Consulting to Management* (Englewood Cliffs, N.J.: Prentice-Hall, 1983), 368 pp.

HOLTZ, HERMAN, *How to Succeed as an Independent Consultant* (New York: Wiley, 1983), 395 pp.

KELLY, ROBERT E., *Consulting: The Complete Guide to a Profitable Career* (New York: Scribner, 1981), 258 pp.

SHENSON, HOWARD L., *How to Strategically Negotiate the Consulting Contract* (Washington, D.C.: Bermont Books, 1980), 107 pp.

STRYKER, STEVEN C., *Guide to Successful Consulting: With Forms, Letters and Checklists* (Englewood Cliffs, N.J.: Prentice-Hall, 1984), 272 pp.

STRYKER, STEVEN C., *Principles and Practices of Professional Consulting* (Washington, D.C.: Consultant's Library, 1982), 149 pp.

APPENDIX B

RATE-SETTING APPROACHES

ALTERNATIVE A: CALCULATING A PER DIEM RATE BASED ON COST, PROFIT, TIME

Expenses (Annual):

Salary/Payment for time (include benefits):

Yours	$ _____
Staff consultant(s)	_____
Research staff	_____
Secretarial	_____
Receptionist	_____
Other _____	_____
_____	_____
Subtotal	$ _____

Space costs:

Rent (or pro rata share
    of house)   _____

Heat   _____

Electric   _____

Other _____   _____

    Subtotal $ _____

Other costs:

Telephone   _____

Copying/Printing (or
    equipment lease)   _____

Insurance

    Premises   _____

    Staff Benefits: Type   _____

Travel (and/or mileage)   _____

Lodging   _____

Business entertainment   _____

Taxes/Employer taxes   _____

Other _____   _____

    Subtotal $ _____

Total annual expenses (estimated) $ _____

One-Time or Infrequent Expenses: (amortize over _____ years)

Organization costs, if any   _____

Stationery/cards   _____

  Logo/Design costs, if any   _____

Security deposits:

  Space   _____

  Electricity   _____

  Telephone   _____

Other _____   _____

Total one-time or infrequent
  expenses $ _____

Calculations

1. Determine costs that need to be covered:

   Divide one-time expenses by amortization period:

        e.g., $30,000/5 years $ _____

   Add total annual expenses   _____

     Total costs to be covered per year $ _____

2. Add desired profit:

   Desired profit percentage   _____ %

   Multiply total costs by profit
     percentage   _____

     Add to total costs for required
       billings amount $ _____

3. Determine probable billable time:

Assuming 250 potential working days
    per consultant, enter percent of time
    that will be billable to clients   _____ %

Multiply percent billable by 250
    days   _____ days

4. Apply billable days to required
    billings:

Divide billable days into total
    required billings amount:
    Per diem rate implied by cost/time
        structure: $ _____
    (round up to the next roundish
        number you like)

ALTERNATIVE B: CALCULATING A PER DIEM RATE BASED ON PROJECT VALUE

This alternative can be used when either the project is intended to save money and the savings can be quantified and/or the perceived value of the project to the purchaser can be estimated in some manner.

1. Estimated value of the project to
    the purchaser: $ _____

Percentage you believe reasonable
    to take in payment: _____ %

Total of your project payment:
    Value × Percent $ _____

2. Estimated professional days required
    to complete project: _____ days

3. Apply required days to total project
   charges:

> Per diem rate implied by
> value/time structure: $ _____
> (round to next roundish number
> you like).

ALTERNATIVE C: FORMULA RATE DEVELOPMENT

This method is frequently used by large partnership operations that
have numerous staff people and equally impressive overheads. It is
rarely usable by small or one-person firms.

   The essential notion is that billings should be allocated one-third
to professional salaries, one-third to overhead, and one-third to partnership profit. The method thus simply takes the annual salary figure,
which you used in Alternative A, and multiplies by 3. This required
revenue figure assumes that your profit and all your other expenses
will be covered by two times your professional salary expense.

1. Annual salary (including fringe
   benefits, bonuses) for
   professional staff members: $ _____

   > Multiply by 3 $ _____

2. Estimate professional days billable to clients:

   > Use figure from Alternative A   _____ days

3. Apply billable days to desired
   revenue/billings:

   > Divide billable days into salaries
   > times 3:
   > Per diem rate implied by
   > formula approach: $ _____

A general note about these methods: As noted in the text, billing rates are partly market dependent. Under any circumstance, however, you will need at least to be able to cover all your expenses (and your personal requirements) from the billings of the business. Thus, it is unwise to use rates calculated under *any* method without checking the results against your calculations in Alternative A. This comment assumes that your own salary and profit (or payment you expect to take out of the business) will cover your personal needs.

APPENDIX C: PROJECT ANALYSIS WORKSHEET

PROJECT ANALYSIS WORKSHEET

PROJECT	SKILL	ROLE	LIKED	DIDN'T	PERF?

CATEGORY

APPENDIX D: PRACTICE OBJECTIVES WORKSHEET

PRACTICE GOALS/OBJECTIVES

SEGMENT	CLIENTS	BILLINGS	BY WHEN?
Business Development:			

INDEX